CHELSEA
100 MEMORABLE MATCHES

CHELSEA CHADDER

Chelsea: 100 Memorable Matches
Copyright: Chelsea Chadder 2018
ISBN: 978-1723964435

Twitter: @ChelseaChadder
Cover photo: © [Cla78] /Adobe Stock
Cover design: Will Hopkins
www.gate17.co.uk

DEDICATION

To Dad,

Thank you for taking me to my first game.

I can see why you love it so much!

GAME 1
Chelsea's first game

Stockport County 1 Chelsea 0
2nd September 1905

Football League Division Two
Edgeley Park
Chelsea; Bill Foulke, Bob Mackie, Robert McEwan, George Key, Bob McRoberts, Thomas Miller, Martin Moran, John Tait Robertson, David Copeland, Jimmy Windridge, Jack Kirwan.
Manager; John Tait Robertson
Referee; D Hammond
Attendance; 7,000

Chelsea's first ever competitive game was a Second Division match away at Stockport County. The Blues were formed half a year earlier at the Rising Sun pub on the 10th March 1905. At the end of May the club had been elected into the league at an AGM, despite some opposition from rival clubs including Tottenham and Fulham.

John Tait Robertson, a Scotland international, was quickly named the club's player/manager. A whole flurry of transfer business took place including the legendary goalkeeper Willy 'Fatty' Foulke who stood at 6ft 4in and weighed around 23 stone. He had recently signed from Sheffield Utd for £50 and was made club captain.

7,000 people attended the match, a record crowd for a Stockport game. The first half was fairly even with both teams going into the break goalless. However, the second half was full of drama. Chelsea conceded a penalty around the hour mark. Foulke managed to save the penalty from Ashton Schofield although Stockport's George Dodd scored from the rebound.

Dodd would later sign for Chelsea six years later, playing 31 times in total.

Chelsea striker Jimmy Windridge went closest to scoring for the Blues after hitting the woodwork twice. Robertson's men were also denied two penalties after Martin Moran was knocked over and a Stockport player handled a shot on the goal line. If only VAR was around back then! It was reported that the referee did consult his linesman but chose not to award a spot kick to the visiting team.

GAME 2
Chelsea's first goal

Blackpool 0 Chelsea 1
9th September 1905

Football League Division Two
Bloomfield Road
Chelsea; Bill Foulke, Bob Mackie, Robert McEwan, George Key, James Watson, John Tait Robertson, Martin Moran, David Copeland, Bob McRoberts, Jimmy Windridge, Jack Kirwan
Scorer; Robertson
Manager; John Tait Robertson
Referee; R Wild
Attendance; 4,000

John Tait Robertson was the young Chelsea player/manager. As a teenager he moved from Scotland to sign with Everton for one season. After that he joined Southampton where he helped the Saints to win the Southern League. Before moving to Chelsea he went back to his home country and won three consecutive league titles with Rangers. The Scottish halfback made his international debut in a loss to England in 1898.

A week after Chelsea played their first ever game they recorded their first ever win. It was a miserable day in terms of weather which didn't help playing conditions on an already bumpy pitch. The game was nearly postponed due to the standing water on the pitch but referee R Wild from Bury gave the game the go ahead.

The Blues made one change to the line-up from the previous game giving a debut to Jack Kirwan. It was George Key in Chelsea's midfield who was causing the most trouble in the first half although Jimmy Windridge's shot was the Blues best effort at goal.

In the second half Chelsea had better luck and more determination to seek out their first ever goal. The game was looking like it would end in a goalless draw until they were awarded a freekick with ten minutes to play. Player/manager John Tait Robertson's strike went through the Blackpool keeper's legs resulting in the club's first competititve goal and win. 4,000 people attended the game but local reporters said it would have been more if not for the weather.

GAME 3
Stamford Bridge debut

Chelsea 5 Hull City 1
11th September 1905

Football League Division Two
Stamford Bridge
Chelsea; Bill Foulke, Bob Mackie, Robert McEwan, George Key, James Watson, John Tait Robertson, Martin Moran, David Copeland, Bob McRoberts, Jimmy Windridge, Jack Kirwan
Scorers; Windridge (3), Copeland (2)
Manager; John Tait Robertson
Referee; F Gardner
Attendance; 6,000

This was Chelsea's first ever competitive game at Stamford Bridge. A week earlier the Blues had beaten Liverpool 4-0 in a friendly to test out the ground. It was 0-0 at half time but second half goals from McRoberts (2), Moran and Windridge gave the home team the win.

A crowd of 6,000 came to see the Blues in action for the Monday match and they would not have been disappointed by what they had seen. A fine display ensured that Chelsea continued their winning ways by beating the visitors 5-1.

It was David Copeland who opened the scoring for the Blues after just 15 minutes. Hull were awarded a penalty but Ambrose Langley's poor spot kick was saved by 'Fatty' Foulke. Chelsea and Copeland doubled their advantage five minutes before half time giving the home side a 2-0 lead at the break.

In the second half Chelsea's Jimmy Windridge scored a brace of his own to make it 4-0 before Peter Howe got a goal back for the visitors. However, Jimmy Windridge scored again to make him the first player to score a hattrick for the Blues. He would later go on to scored 58 goals for Chelsea in 152 games. Things were really looking good for the team as they looked to gain promotion in their first season.

GAME 4
A scoring debut

Leicester 0 Chelsea 1
30th September 1905

Football League Division Two
Filbert Street
Chelsea; Bill Foulke, Bob Mackie, Robert McEwan, George Key, James Watson, John Tait Robertson, Martin Moran, James Robertson, David Copeland, Jimmy Windridge, Jack Kirwan
Scorer; James Robertson
Manager; John Tait Robertson
Referee; JH Strawson
Attendance; 7,000

James Robertson was an inside right who moved from Scotland to play for Crewe. His goalscoring ability attracted the attention of Small Heath who had recently been promoted to the First Division. However, he wasn't able to fulfill his potential and in 1905 he signed for Chelsea alongside Jimmy Windridge and Bob McRoberts.

Although Windridge and McRoberts had played in the Blues opening fixture, Robertson had to wait until the end of September to make his debut. By that time 12 players had made their first Chelsea appearance. A total of 28 different players made the starting XI that season but it was Robertson's that created a piece of history.

Chelsea travelled to Filbert Street to face Leicester. Manager John Tait Robertson (no relation to James) made one change from the previous game, a 1-0 win against West Brom. Bob McRoberts had scored the goal but was replaced by James Robertson for the match against the Foxes.

James Robertson repaid his manager's decision to give him his debut as his solitary goal after ten minutes made him the first player to score for Chelsea on their debut. Many have gone on to achieve this feat including the likes of Jimmy Greaves, Bobby Tambling, Peter Osgood, Kerry Dixon, Jimmy Floyd Hasselbaink and Diego Costa.

By the end of his Blues career Robertson had scored 21 goals in 28 games before moving to Glossop in 1907. He later signed for Leyton, Partick Thistle, Ayr United and Leeds City. The Scottish attacker retired in 1915.

GAME 5
No goalkeeper

Southern Utd 0 Chelsea 1
28th October 1905

FA Cup Preliminary Round 2
Nunhead
Chelsea; Bob Mackie, James Watson, Robert McEwan, George Key, Bob McRoberts, John Tait Robertson, Martin Moran, Tommy McDermott, Frank Pearson, Jimmy Windridge, Joe Goodwin
Scorer; McDermott
Manager; John Tait Robertson
Referee; CC Fallowfield
Attendance; 7,000

Willy 'Fatty' Foulke had played around 300 games for Sheffield Utd and played in three FA Cup finals, winning two of them and a First Division title. He had also been capped once by England against Wales in 1897. He had a temperamental side and intimidated players and officials alike.

Chelsea travelled to Nunhead to play in the FA Cup. The Blues had beat 1st Grenadiers 6-1 in the previous preliminary round of the FA Cup courtesy of goals from Francis O'Hara (2), Jimmy Windridge (2), James Robertson and Martin Moran. Chelsea's captain and goalkeeper Willy Foulke was absent for the game and so Bob Mackie, a Scottish fullback deputised in goal for the day. He was the first outfield player to go in goal.

The Blues managed to beat Southern Utd 1-0 thanks to Tom McDermott who scored the only goal of the game. His strike after half an hour ensured Chelsea would reach the next round of the cup and recorded the club's first ever clean sheet in the FA Cup.

The next round of the cup saw Chelsea lose 7-1 to Crystal Palace. This match was scheduled on the same day that the Blues had a league match vs Burnley at the same time! As the league was a priority a reserve side was fielded in the cup giving debuts to five players including Frank Wolff and Walter Toomer who made their only appearances for the club. In better news, Chelsea won their league game 1-0 vs Burnley with Bob McRoberts getting the goal and pushing the club into third place in the table.

Foulkes left the Blues at the end of the season and died ten years later. Bob Mackie made 48 appearances over three seasons scoring just one goal, in his debut season, vs Gainsborough Trinity in a 3-1 home defeat.

GAME 6
The first promotion

Chelsea 4 Gainsborough Trinity 1
27th April 1907

Football League Division Two
Stamford Bridge
Chelsea; Bob Whiting, Joseph Walton, Thomas Miller, George Henderson, George Key, Peter Proudfoot, Martin Moran, William Bridgeman, George Hilsdon, Jimmy Windridge, Jack Kirwan
Scorers; Windridge (3), Hilsdon
Manager; William Lewis
Referee; H Pollitt
Attendance; 15,000

In Chelsea's debut season the club missed out on promotion by finishing third behind Manchester Utd and champions Bristol City despite being the division's top goal scorers. The club were moving in the right direction and started off the new season well.

In November John Tait Robertson had guided Chelsea to third in the table after beating Barnsley 2-1 at the Bridge in front of a crowd of 14,000. The Blues player/manager suddenly and surprisingly resigned leaving the club without a manager. Club secretary William Lewis became caretaker manager until the end of the season.

Chelsea had fought long and hard that season and had managed to seal promotion into the First Division at the second time of asking. The final game of the season started off well as Jimmy Windridge gave the Blues the lead after just 15 minutes. He doubled Chelsea's advantage just before the half hour mark and a George Hilsdon penalty gave them a 3-0 lead at half time.

The second half saw a confident Chelsea side with Windridge claiming another hattrick to make the score 4-0. The visitors did get a consolation goal back in the 80th minute through Joseph Kitchen but his goal was not enough to dampen the home side's mood as they were ready to ply their trade in England's top division.

GAME 7
A double hattrick

Chelsea 9 Worksop Town 1
11th January 1908

FA Cup Round 1
Stamford Bridge
Chelsea; Jack Whitley, Jock Cameron, Augustus Harding, George Henderson, James Stark, Ted Birnie, Billy Brawn, Ben Whitehouse, George Hilsdon, Jimmy Windridge, William Bridgeman
Scorers; Hilsdon (6), Windridge (2), Bridgeman
Manager; David Calderhead
Referee; JW Bailey
Attendance; 18,995

Regular visitors to Stamford Bridge will have seen many changes over the years including removing the running track around the pitch, completely rebuilding whole stands and having a more branded and corporate feel. In days gone by, overlooking the stadium, was a weather vane modelled on former Chelsea striker George 'Gattling Gun' Hilsdon.

Hilsdon was an English striker who began his career at West Ham before transferring to the Blues in 1906, earning £4 a week. A year later he made his international debut against Ireland. Although he was only capped eight times the Chelsea striker managed to score 14 goals.

In the previous season the Blues beat Glossop 9-2 on the opening day of the season with Hilsdon scoring five times on his debut. A year later the Londoners thrashed Nottinghamshire club Worksop Town 9-1. Chelsea were drawn away in this cup fixture but the game was played at Stamford Bridge by appointment.

It was Hilsdon who opened the scoring after quarter of an hour with Jimmy Windridge adding another a minute later. The Blues were 4-1 up at half time with Billy Bridgeman and Windridge scoring either side of a goal by Richardson for the 'visitors'. Most teams may have taken their foot off the gas but not this Blues side, or Hilsdon especially. It was the England international that scored in the first minute of the second half and then went on to score another four goals that half taking his tally to six! This was the first (and only) time a Chelsea player has netted a double hattrick.

GAME 8
A record crowd

Chelsea 2 Newcastle 1
27th December 1909

Football League Division One
Stamford Bridge
Chelsea; James Saunders, Wally Bettridge, Bill Cartwright, Frederick Taylor, Ted Birnie, Sam Downing, Billy Brawn, Vivian Woodward, Evan Jones, Jimmy Windridge, Ernest Williams
Scorers; Brawn, Woodward
Manager; David Calderhead
Referee; J Sykes
Attendance; 70,000

Towards the end of the decade Chelsea were becoming one of the most popular teams to watch in the land, regularly entertaining crowds over 20,000. However, two days after Christmas Day the Blues took on Newcastle Utd at The Bridge. Festive fever was clearly in the air as 70,000 people came to watch the game, the largest ever crowd to watch a league match in England at that time.

Newcastle took the lead in the first half when Colin Veitch scored just before the half hour mark. Billy Brawn did level things before half time and it was the home side that pressed on and sealed victory courtesy of a goal by Vivian Woodward. Chelsea had become the club of choice to watch.

Almost 25 years later Chelsea surpassed the 70,000 attendance at Stamford Bridge when they welcomed Arsenal in 1935. The crowd was reported as 82,905. The game ended 1-1 with the Blues taking the lead through Joe Bambrick before Jack Crayston equalised for the Gooners. Due to Stamford

Bridge being required to be an all seater stadium there is very little chance this attendance will be beaten unless they move to a new home, whether permanently or temporarily.

GAME 9
A sending off

Nottingham Forest 0 Chelsea 0
5th March 1910

Football League Division One
The City Ground
Chelsea; Jack Whitley, Bill Cartwright, Jock Cameron, Frederick Taylor, Andy Ormiston, Sam Downing, Angus Douglas, Vivian Woodward, George Hilsdon, Jimmy Windridge, Arthur Holden
Sent off; Windridge
Manager; David Calderhead
Referee; A Briggs
Attendance; 7,000

Jimmy Windridge was an inside forward who signed for Chelsea in their inaugural season from Small Heath for a fee of £190. He scored 16 goals in his first season at the Bridge. This was followed up by 18 more in the next campaign. His talent was recognised and was given his first England cap vs Ireland in 1908. Windridge scored in six consecutive internationals which is an England record that has not been beaten since.

It's not often that a 0-0 game can generate any memorable moments, especially for a team fighting the relegation battle. So why does this game feature in the book?

Chelsea's striker Jimmy Windridge landed himself with a milestone that is probably one he would care to forget. The England International was given his marching orders as he became the first ever CFC player to be sent off in a match. There may have been some consolation that the opposition's George Needham was also dismissed from the game. Windridge left the club the following year to join Middlesbrough.

GAME 10
The first relegation

Tottenham 2 Chelsea 1
30th April 1910

Football League Division One
White Hart Lane
Chelsea; Jack Whitley, Bill Cartwright, Jock Cameron, Frederick Taylor, English McConnell, Sam Downing, Angus Douglas, Bob Whittingham, Vivian Woodward, Jimmy Windridge, Marshall McEwan
Scorer; Windridge
Manager; David Calderhead
Referee; R Horrocks
Attendance; 35,000

Every football fan will experience the highs and lows that the game can bring. Chelsea are a club who in more recent years have given fans more joy than most could ever imagine. Some may take it for granted but on the 30th of April 1910 the Blues suffered real heartache for the first time.

A week earlier Woolwich Arsenal lost their final game of the season 3-1 at home to Preston North End leaving them just two points above Chelsea. The Blues still had one game to play against North London rivals Tottenham knowing that only a win would help them stay in England's top division and avoid relegation.

Chelsea started well with Jimmy Windridge giving them an early lead with a goal after just five minutes. Tottenham did manage to get a goal back just before half time setting up a nail biting second half. Spurs took the advantage as Percy Humphreys netted in the 57th minute. This gave the Blues half an hour to mount a fight back and save their season.

Unfortunately, it was not to be and the 2-1 loss ensured that the club would be relegated, alongside Bolton Wanderers, for the first time in their history.

GAME 11
A century of goals

Stockport County 2 Chelsea 2
2nd January 1911

Football League Division Two
Edgeley Park
Chelsea; James Molyneux, Wally Bettridge, Bill Cartwright, Frederick Taylor, Ben Warren, Sam Downing, Angus Douglas, Bob Whittingham, George Hilsdon, Charlie Freeman, Marshall McEwan
Scorers; Hilsdon, Whittingham
Manager; David Calderhead
Referee; James Mason
Attendance; 5,000

Another game vs Stockport and another that creates some more Chelsea history. Just over five years after their first ever game the Blues returned to Edgeley Park but this time managed to leave the ground with a point.

Bob Whittingham gave Chelsea the lead after his goal beat Stockport's keeper Ted Price after 25 minutes. The home side did level the score shortly before half time. In the second half it was Stockport who took the lead with only seven minutes to go, surely giving them the win. But the Blues fought on until the end and it was George Hilsdon who became the hero as his goal three minutes from time gave them a much needed point in their push for promotion.

Hilsdon must have been pleased to earn a draw for his team especially as he became the first Chelsea player to score 100 goals for the Blues. The striker went on to score another nine goals taking his final tally to 109 before transferring back to former club West Ham.

During the first World War Hilsdon tried to avoid active service by hiding in a chicken run but was found by police and sent to fight. He fell victim to a gas attack that caused so much damage that it ended his football career. After this he had a variety of jobs before his death in 1941. It was reported that only four people attended his funeral but in 2015 Chelsea fans raised funds to pay for a headstone for their former hero.

GAME 12
The first overseas player

Chelsea 2 Derby 1
15th November 1913

Football League Division One
Stamford Bridge
Chelsea; James Molyneux, Owen Marshall, James Sharp, Frederick Taylor, Nils Middelboe, George Hunter, Harry Ford, Harold Halse, Bob Whittingham, Charlie Freeman, Norman Fairgray
Scorers; Freeman, Whittingham
Manager; David Calderhead
Referee; S D Peers
Attendance; 28,000

Eden Hazard, Didier Drogba and Gianfranco Zola are names that will go down in history as some of the greatest players to put on a Chelsea shirt. Their route into the club was no different than the majority of signings made by English clubs. However, there is one name that should also be remembered as fondly for paving the way for these superstars.

Nils Middelboe became the first overseas player to put on a CFC shirt. He was an unknown amateur athlete and international footballer. Middleboe had won silver medals at the 1908 and 1912 Olympic Games, losing to Britain and England respectively. The Dane did actually sign from Newcastle although never played a game for the Magpies. He was a Danish triple jump and four x 100 metres relay champion, and set Danish records in the 800 metres and triple jump.

Fans at the game may have been surprised by his inclusion in the team, especially when he was named captain for the game. His teammates had appointed him as skipper as a show of faith. It may have just been beginners luck but the Blues won the game with goals from Charlie Freeman and Bob Whittingham before James Henry 'Harry' Walker scored a consolation goal for the visitors.

GAME 13
The first FA Cup final

Chelsea 0 Sheffield Utd 3
24th April 1915

FA Cup Final
Old Trafford
Chelsea; James Molyneux, Wally Bettridge, Jack Harrow, Frederick Taylor, Tom Logan, Andrew Walker, Harry Ford, Harold Halse, Robert Thomson, Jimmy Croal, Bob McNeil
Manager; David Calderhead
Referee; HH Taylor
Attendance; 49,557

In recent years Chelsea have had a lot of success in cup competitions, especially the FA Cup. In 1911 the Blues did make it to the semi final stage despite being in the Second Division. They managed to go one better than that in the 1914-15 season after beating Everton 2-0 at Villa Park courtesy of second half goals from Harold Halse and Jimmy Croal. Their reward was a cup final meeting with Sheffield Utd.

The end of season show piece would be the last FA Cup game before competitive football was suspended in Britain due to WW1. The game was usually played at Crystal Palace but the venue was changed to Old Trafford to avoid disruption to travel in the capital.

The game was often referred to as the Khaki Cup Final due to large number of uniformed soldiers in attendance. The crowd for the game was 50,000 which was lower than previous years. Again, this was due to war time restrictions of movement and the fact that many young men had joined the armed forces.

The favourites to win the cup were Sheffield Utd. They finished sixth in the league, just three points behind the eventual winners, Everton. In contrast, the Blues finished one place off the bottom of the division although did manage to score more league goals that season than the Blades.

Chelsea's leading goalscorer that season was Bob Thomson but he had been injured in a recent game against Bolton ten days earlier. His fitness for the game was in doubt but England international Vivian Woodward was available for selection after being given leave by the British army to play in the game. Woodward was loyal to his teammates and insisted that Thomson should play in the final rather than himself as he had helped them reach the final.

Sheffield Utd took a 1-0 lead just before half time after Jimmy Simmons volleyed the ball into the net via a cross from the left hand side. The second half became unwatchable, not for the quality of football rather the thick blanket of fog that descended over the pitch. A headed goal by Stan Fazackerley and a cool finish by Joseph Kitchen sealed a 3-0 victory for the Blades.

GAME 14
An overseas goalscorer

Chelsea 4 Preston 0
15th November 1919

Football League Division One
Stamford Bridge
Chelsea; Colin Hampton, Wally Bettridge, Jack Harrow, Nils Middelboe, Harry Wilding, Tom Logan, George Dale, Harold Halse, Jack Cock, Jimmy Croal, Bob McNeil
Scorers; Cock (3), Middelboe
Manager; David Calderhead
Referee; J F Pearson
Attendance; 34,000

Exactly six years before this game Nils Middelboe became the first overseas player to make his Chelsea debut. Due to the outbreak of the war competitive football in Britain was put on hold but the Great Dane used this time to qualify as a lawyer and managed to secure employment in a London bank.

When football commenced after WW1 he wanted to pursue his new career despite the fact he would have earned more money as a footballer. Middelboe didn't want the football to interfere with this too much so an agreement was made that he was not required to travel to away games.

Although Middelboe was considered a defensive midfielder he did score seven goals for his country in just 15 appearances. He had the honour of scoring Denmark's first ever goal in their debut game at the 1908 Olympics. In fact, it was the first ever goal scored by an official national team in Olympic football when he netted against France. However, he set another milestone for his club side. Nils Middelboe became the first overseas player to score for Chelsea.

The Blues beat Preston 4-0 and it was Middelboe who opened the scoring after just ten minutes. A second half hattrick from Jack Cock gave Chelsea the win in front of a crowd of 34,000 at Stamford Bridge.

The Great Dane returned to his homeland in 1936. He led his KB side to the championship title in 1940. After WW2 a friendly was arranged between Chelsea and KB to celebrate the club's 70th anniversary. The Blues lost 2-1 in that game.

GAME 15
A goalkeeper on the scoresheet

Chelsea 1 Bradford City 0
19th November 1921

Football League Division One
Stamford Bridge
Chelsea; Ben Howard Baker, Jack Harrow, George Smith, Tommy Meehan, Ken McKenzie, Stephen Smith, Dr. John Bell, Frank Hoddinott, Jack Cock, Jimmy Croal, Bob McNeil
Scorer; Baker
Manager; David Calderhead
Referee; S Rothwell
Attendance; 35,000

Chelsea have signed many superstars over the years and back in October 1921 the Blues signed England goalkeeper Ben Howard Baker. He is one of the most gifted sportsman in the club's history. As well as being an international footballer he also excelled in many other sports. He represented his country at water polo and held the British records for high jump and triple jump. Baker took part in the 1912 and 1920 Olympics in these sports but failed to win a medal.

One month after signing for the club a crowd of 35,000 came to watch the Blues entertain Bradford City at Stamford Bridge. A relatively dull first half ensured that both teams headed into the break at 0-0. The game looked like it would be a stalemate until the last five minutes Chelsea won a penalty. They had missed the two previous penalties they had been awarded and so a new spot kick taker emerged. It was non other than Baker, the Blues goalkeeper. His shot managed to beat Bradford's Jock Ewart and ensured that Chelsea won the game.

So, apart from his major sporting achievements Ben Howard Baker can add the honour of being the first goalkeeper to score for Chelsea.

GAME 16
Top of the league

Birmingham 0 Chelsea 1
2nd September 1922

Football League Division One

St Andrews

Chelsea; Ben Howard Baker, George Smith, Jack Harrow, Harry Wilding, David Cameron, Tommy Meehan, William Haywood, Harry Ford, Jack Cock, Buchanan Sharp, Bob McNeil

Scorer; Sharp

Manager; David Calderhead

Referee; J G A Sharpe

Attendance; 35,000

Chelsea ended the 1921/22 season finishing in ninth place but only two points away from third placed Burnley. However, they started the 1922/23 season with a bang. Their opening day fixture saw the Blues earn a 1-1 at home to Birmingham courtesy of a late goal from John Bell. Chelsea then beat Stoke 2-1 away with Buchanan Sharp scoring a brace.

The third game of the season involved Chelsea travelling to play Birmingham, hoping to continue their early unbeaten run. Despite a goalless first half it was Buchanan Sharp who popped up and scored the only goal of the game. This result meant that Chelsea sat top of the league for the first time in their history. They remained there for their next two games but inconsistent results saw the Blues end the season with a disappointing 19th place finish.

GAME 17
A thousand Chelsea goals

Middlebrough 1 Chelsea 2
12th December 1925

Football League Division Two
Ayresome Park
Chelsea; Peter McKenna, George Smith, Fred Barrett, John Priestley, George Rodger, Willie Ferguson, Jackie Crawford, Albert Thain, Bob Turnbull, Andy Wilson, Bob McNeil
Scorers; Turnbull, Barrett
Manager; David Calderhead
Referee; W E Forshaw
Attendance; 14,395

In 1925/26 Chelsea were in the Second Division but doing well. The Blues were pushing for promotion back into the top flight after being relegated two seasons prior. They had been an established club in the football league for 20 years playing just over 700 matches in that time.

That season Chelsea earn a 1-1 draw with Stoke at Stamford Bridge. Albert Thain gave the home side a 1-0 lead early in the second half before Harry Davies levelled the scores with only ten minutes remaining. The strike by Thain was the Blues 999th goal in all competitions.

On Saturday the 12th December 1925 Chelsea were looking to get their first win in four games and score their 1,000th goal in the process. Things were tight between the two sides and went in 0-0 at the break. It was Middlesbrough who took the lead after 65 minutes with a goal by the outside left Owen Williams who had been capped by England a few years before. However, five minutes later Bob Turnbull netted to give the Blues an equaliser and the 1,000th goal in their history. Even better for the home side was that fullback Fred Barrett scored his first ever goal in a Chelsea shirt with only minutes left on the clock. Andy Wilson also missed a penalty for Chelsea in the game but the Blues would hold on to the victory and be up to second in the table.

GAME 18
Shirt numbers

Chelsea 4 Swansea 0
25th August 1928

Football League Division Two
Stamford Bridge
Chelsea; Sam Millington, George Smith, Tommy Law, Sam Irving, John Townrow, Sid Bishop, Jackie Crawford, George Biswell, Sidney Elliot, Andy Wilson, George Pearson
Scorers; Elliot, Crawford, Pearson, Biswell
Manager; David Calderhead
Referee; A J Caseley
Attendance; 47,264

In the 1993/94 season the Premier League introduced squad numbers. This meant that players had to wear the same number the whole season. Some shirt numbers have become synonymous with Chelsea players such as 25 for Gianfranco Zola and 26 for John Terry. Before squad numbers players would wear 1 to 11 on the back of their shirts with substitutes numbered 12 and above. Squad numbers have helped with branding as well as easily recognising players on the pitch.

In the early years of Chelsea's history all shirts were blank. No numbers, and certainly no names, could be seen. It wasn't until the 1920's when this changed. It was the Blues, along with Arsenal, who debuted the idea of shirt numbers.

On the 25th of August 1928 the football season kicked off. Chelsea welcomed Swansea to Stamford Bridge. Fans were intrigued by the concept of shirt numbering but it was a lot easier to follow the action, especially for new fans or those watching from the back of the stands. It was only outfield players who wore a number on their shirt which were large black numbers on white squares.

It could have been argued that it would have made it easier for the opposition to keep a track of their man but this clearly wasn't the case for Swansea. Chelsea were 1-0 up in the first half through Sidney Elliot. Three more goals in the second half from Jackie Crawford, George Pearson and George Biswell made it 4-0.

GAME 19
Playing under floodlights

Rio de Janeiro XI 1 Chelsea 1
28th June 1929

Friendly
Ru Guanabara Stadium
Chelsea; Sam Millington, George Smith, Leslie Odell, Sid Bishop, Jack Townrow, Willie Ferguson, Billy Jackson, Jackie Crawford, Reg Weaver, Harold Miller, George Pearson
Scorer; Jackson
Manager; David Calderhead
Referee; L Moraes Castro
Attendance; 45,000

In 1929 Chelsea undertook a tour of South America playing a variety of teams from Brazil, Argentina and Uruguay. During the tour the Blues would earn the nickname Los Numerados (the numbered ones) due to the fact that Chelsea wore numbered shirts. This was not common practice in the English football league until ten years later.

The tour started with a 3-2 win over a Buenos Aires XI with goals from Harold Miller, Jackie Crawford and a winning strike by Sidney Elliot. However, Chelsea only won three of their next 11 games. There were only four games remaining until they would jet off back home before playing against Rio de Janeiro XI on the 28th of June 1929.

A crowd of 45,000 people had come to watch this friendly which ended in a 1-1 draw. Chelsea took the lead through William Jackson just before half time. It was only a goal by Rio in the last ten minutes of the game that stopped the Blues winning the game.

Although the match itself may not be memorable for the quality of the play it was a first in Chelsea history. This game saw the Blues make their debut in a game that used floodlights. All previous matches had been played during the day time but this once novel idea has now become so important in making football a world game.

GAME 20
Calderhead's curtain call

Chelsea 1 Sunderland 1
6th May 1933

Football League Division One
Stamford Bridge

Chelsea; Vic Woodley, George Barber, Bob MacAulay, William Russell, Peter O'Dowd, Allan Craig, Eric Oakton, George Mills, Hughie Gallacher, George Gibson, Jack Horton

Scorer; Gibson
Manager; David Calderhead
Referee; W Booth
Attendance; 22,322

The career of a football manager in today's game is full of pressure where instant and constant success is the only currency football clubs want. There have been few managers in recent years that have managed to last longer than three seasons before getting the boot. It's also been known that some managers last less than a season and the managerial merry-go-round at Chelsea in recent years has become the norm.

John Tait Robertson was Chelsea's first manager but he left part way through his second season. It left to William Lewis, the club secretary, who became the caretaker manager until the end of the campaign to take charge. In his 27 games in charge he guided the Blues to their first promotion before stepping down.

In 1900 a former Scottish international joined Lincoln City and became their manager. His name was David Calderhead. It was seven years later when his team welcomed Chelsea to Sincil Bank for an FA Cup game. The Blues looked to be in the draw for the next round after leading 2-0 but two goals in the final few minutes earned Lincoln a replay at Stamford Bridge. After 90 minutes of the replay the score was goalless until Lincoln's Norman Fairgray scored the winner. Calderhead's victory had alerted the Blues board to his talent and in the summer they secured his services as manager. Calderhead brought over Fairgray to join him at the club.

David Calderhead started his Chelsea career with a 4-2 home defeat against Sheffield United, followed by losses to Newcastle (1-0) and Nottingham Forest (6-0). By the end of the season he had seen a turn of form and finished in 13th place. After eight years as the Blues boss he took them to their first FA Cup final but lost 3-0. Despite this, the Chelsea board kept faith with their man.

The Blues boss was notoriously shy of the media and was labelled the 'Sphinx of Stamford Bridge'. However, he did let his actions do the talking. He spent big money on a host a strikers including Hughie Gallacher, Alex Jackson and Alec Cheyne. He also gave a debut to his son, also called David, who went on to play 43 times over four seasons.

On the 6th of May 1933 Chelsea welcomed Sunderland to Stamford Bridge for the final game of the season. The Blues were hovering near the relegation zone but had guaranteed their survival going into the game. The first half ended goalless but Chelsea's George Gibson put his side ahead. This was until a quirk of interest meant that Sunderland equalised by their own George Gibson. After 90 minutes the match finished 1-1 but something bigger also had come to an end.

This game was to be David Calderhead's final game in charge before he was replaced by Leslie Knighton two days later. He joined the club in 1907 and had been manager for a record 966 matches. His career stats were W385, D239 and L342. It is doubtful that his career will be surpassed at Chelsea in terms of longevity and should be remembered for his time at the club.

Sadly, the Scotsman died five years later at the age of 73.

GAME 21
The Russians are coming

Chelsea 3 Dynamo Moscow 3
13th November 1945

Friendly

Stamford Bridge

Chelsea; Vic Woodley, Albert Tennant, Joe Bacuzzi, Bob Russell, John Harris, Jim Taylor, Peter Buchanan, Reg Williams, Tommy Lawton, Len Goulden, Jimmy Bain

Scorers; Williams, Goulden, Lawton

Manager; Billy Birrell

Referee; G Clark

Attendance; 74,496

The start of WW2 in 1939 put a hold on all competitive football in England. Although teams still competed in various competitions none of them are ever noted in the record books. During the war a lot of young men went to fight for their country and so that would naturally include some of the top footballers of their day. This meant that a lot of teams fielded a starting XI with guest players from other teams.

After the war ended in 1945 football tried to get back to where it left off. This was not that easy as many footballers had lost their lives or were injured in battle. Some just felt they were too old to compete and had retired. One thing that hadn't changed was the love of the game that many fans and players wanted to enjoy again.

In November 1945 Dynamo Moscow from Russia were invited to Britain by the English FA as they were intrigued by the nature of football behind the Iron Curtain. A series of games were scheduled including a match against

Chelsea at Stamford Bridge.

The official attendance was 74,496 but a reported crowd of over 100,000 came to watch the game between Chelsea and their WW2 allies from Russia. Before the game the Moscow side came out early and starting warming up which was something new to English football. Also, every Blues player was handed a wreath of flowers which was normal practice in the visitor's home country. This was also a special occasion for Tommy Lawton as he had only recently joined Chelsea for a record sum of £115,000 from Everton a week earlier.

The match started well for Chelsea, wearing red due to a clash in kits, as they went into the half time break winning 2-0 with goals coming from Len Goulden and Reg Williams. With 20 minutes to go Dynamo Moscow pulled a goal back through Vassili Kartsev before Evgeny Archangelski equalised for the visitors. It was record signing Tommy Lawton who appeared to have won the game for Chelsea with a header until Vsevolod Bobrov scored just minutes later. It was reported that the crowd were delighted in seeing the Russians equalise despite Bobrov being five yards offside. The referee apparently told Lawton that he allowed the goal to stand for 'diplomatic reasons'.

GAME 22
Surviving relegation by less than a goal

Chelsea 4 Bolton 0
5th May 1951

Football League Division One
Stamford Bridge
Chelsea; Bill Robertson, Sid Bathgate, Sid Tickridge, Bill Dickson, Jack Saunders, Frank Mitchell, Bobby Campbell, Roy Bentley, Bobby Smith, Ken Armstrong, Billy Gray
Scorers; Bentley (2), Smith (2)
Booked; Mitchell
Manager; Billy Birrell
Referee; G L Iliffe
Attendance; 38,928

Back in 1951 things were not looking good for Chelsea. On the 18th of April the Blues lost away to Huddersfield leaving the club winless in 15 games. This result left them bottom of the table and six points from safety in a time when you only got two points for a win. Not only that but there were only four matches left to play.

Chelsea managed to get their first win since the end of January after beating Liverpool 1-0 at Stamford Bridge. This was followed by further wins vs Wolves and Fulham, both by the same 2-1 score line after going a goal behind. There was hope for the Blues yet as Everton and Sheffield Wednesday, who Chelsea were trying to catch to survive the drop, were both on a run of bad results.

The last day of the season saw Everton take on Sheffield Wednesday. A win for Everton would mean both Chelsea and Wednesday would be playing in the Second Division next year. In a weird twist of fate it was Wednesday who thrashed Everton 6-0. This put them equal on points with the Merseysiders and saw them go above them on goal average. This was based on goals scored divided by goals against in the days before goal difference being a deciding factor. The Sheffield side had a goal average of 0.771. This meant that not only did Chelsea have to win to have a chance of staying up but they needed to win by two or more goals.

The day started off fantastically as Roy Bentley scored just after the 15 minute mark and then doubled his tally a couple of minutes later. Bobby Smith then made it 3-0 to Chelsea five minutes before half time. It was Smith who also scored a brace giving Chelsea a 4-0 win and saw the Blues escape relegation by 0.044 of a goal.

GAME 23
A unique own goal

Chelsea 3 Leicester 1
18th December 1954

Football League Division One
Stamford Bridge
Chelsea; Bill Robertson, John Harris, Peter Sillett, Ken Armstrong, Ron Greenwood, Derek Saunders, Eric Parsons, Johnny McNichol, Roy Bentley, Les Stubbs, Frank Blunstone
Scorers; Parsons, McNichol, Milburn & Froggatt (O.G)
Manager; Ted Drake
Referee; Arthur Edward Ellis
Attendance; 33,215

1954/55 was the 50th anniversary season for Chelsea having been formed half a century ago. The Blues finished eighth in the previous campaign which was a huge improvement from the 19th, 19th and 20th placed finishes before that.

The season did not start off well with only five wins in seventeen games. Things picked up in November and by the time they faced Leicester at Stamford Bridge a week before Christmas the Blues were up to fourth in the table. Chelsea had won their last three games scoring four goals in each game with Roy Bentley, Johnny McNichol and Les Stubbs netting the majority of goals.

On the 18th of December 1954 the Blues welcomed Leicester to Stamford Bridge. This game saw the home side continue their winning run but something special happened in this game that had never been recorded before or since. Chelsea had taken the lead when Eric Parsons put them in front after 15 minutes. Ten minutes later the Blues were on the attack again, Leicester's Stan Milburn and Jack Froggatt went to clear a ball but simultaneously kicked it into their own net. As nobody could determine who got the final touch it was decided that it would be credited as a joint own goal.

Chelsea went on to win 3-1 when Johnny McNichol added a third just before Andy Graver scored a consolation goal for Leicester. Roy Bentley also had a penalty saved in the game.

GAME 24
Champions!

Chelsea 3 Sheffield Wednesday 0
23rd April 1955

Football League Division One
Stamford Bridge
Chelsea; Chick Thomson, Peter Sillett, Stan Willemse, Ken Armstrong, Stan Wicks, Derek Saunders, Eric Parsons, Johnny McNichol, Roy Bentley, Seamus O'Connell, Frank Blunstone
Scorers; Parsons (2), Sillett
Manager; Ted Drake
Referee; William Ling
Attendance; 51,421

This would become the most memorable and celebrated day in Chelsea's 50 year history. The Blues had put together a tremendous run in the second half of the season and saw them top of the league in April. With just four games to go they were five points clear of nearest rivals Wolves and Portsmouth who both had three games in hand on Chelsea. The next two fixtures for the Londoners were against Wolves and Portsmouth!

The match against Wolves on Easter Sunday saw a Peter Sillett penalty win the game at Stamford Bridge which was followed by a goalless draw at Fratton Park vs Pompey. Now there were just two games left to play and Chelsea only needed to beat already relegated Sheffield Wednesday and hope that Portsmouth would fail to beat Cardiff City to seal their first ever league title.

A crowd of over 51,000 came to Stamford Bridge to see if the Blues could be crowned the champions of England. Chelsea made one change to their starting line up with Seamus O'Connell replacing Les Stubbs on the teamsheet.

It was Eric Parsons who headed the home side in front after just 23 minutes and this would be the only goal of the first half. In the final 45 minutes Chelsea were awarded a penalty which Peter Sillett calmly converted before Parsons doubled his tally ensuring a 3-0 win for the Blues. Meanwhile, Cardiff City managed to hold Portsmouth to a 1-1 draw confirming Chelsea would be champions with one game left to play. Chelsea captain Roy Bentley gave a speech to the crowd thanking them on behalf of the players which ended with a huge roar from the Stamford Bridge faithful.

GAME 25
The longest FA Cup tie

Chelsea 2 Burnley 0
15th February 1956

FA Cup Round 4 (replay)

White Hart Lane

Chelsea; Chick Thomson, Peter Sillett, Stan Willemse, Brian Nicholas, Bill Livingstone, Derek Saunders, Jim Lewis, Johnny McNichol, Roy Bentley, Ron Tindall, Frank Blunstone

Scorers; Tindall, Lewis

Manager; Ted Drake

Referee; Leo Callaghan

Attendance; 27,210

A year after winning the league Chelsea were looking to build on their success by mounting a good cup run. The Blues started their FA Cup campaign with a match against Hartlepool Utd at Victoria Park in the third round. It was Chelsea who managed to get a 1-0 victory courtesy of an own goal by Hartlepool's Watty Moore.

In the next round they were paired with Burnley. A crowd of just under 45,000 saw Burnley take an early lead at Turf Moor and looked to be heading into the next round until Eric Parsons equalised in the last ten minutes. No further goals were scored and so a replay was arranged at Stamford Bridge three days later. Frank Blunstone gave the home side the advantage with his goal in the 55th minute but this was cancelled out by Brian Pilkington who scored with twenty minutes left to play.

As was standard practice a further replay was played but at a neutral venue. This time Birmingham's St Andrews was used. Just like the previous ties the game was back and forth with Burnley taking the lead twice through goals from Peter McKay and Jimmy McIlroy. Peter Sillett scored inbetween these goals and Roy Bentley netted with 15 minutes to go to make it 2-2. A further replay was then scheduled two days later but this time closer to Chelsea with a match played at Arsenal's Highbury.

In the fourth FA Cup match between Chelsea and Burnley the scores were level after 90 minutes and so an additional 30 minutes extra time were played to try to find a winner. Unbelievably the score remained goalless and a fifth match to determine who progressed into the fifth round against Everton at Goodison Park was needed.

On Wednesday 15th February Chelsea and Burnley competed in an FA Cup 4th round replay for the fourth time, at Tottenham's White Hart Lane. The Blues took the lead through Ron Tindall after 36 minutes. With ten minutes left to play Jim Lewis doubled Chelsea's advantage before referee Leo Callaghan blew his whistle to signal the end of the match and a gruelling FA Cup tie lasting eight and a half hours. This was the Blues longest running cup tie ever.

GAME 26
Stamford Bridge under the lights

Chelsea 2 Sparta 0
19th March 1957

Friendly
Stamford Bridge
Chelsea; Reg Matthews, Dick Whittaker, Peter Sillett, John Mortimore, Alan Dicks, Derek Saunders, Peter Brabrook, John McNichol, Les Allen, Derek Gibbs, Bobby Laverick
Scorers; Allen, Gibbs
Manager; Ted Drake
Attendance; 30,701

In 1957 Chelsea entertained Sparta, the reigning champions of Czechoslovakia in a friendly at Stamford Bridge. What made this game memorable was that this was the first time the Blues used floodlights in a game at home. Just over 30,000 people attended the game with the artificial lighting towering 170 feet above the pitch. The lights were actually tested the night before when a Chelsea juniors side played in a private match.

Les Allen (father of future Chelsea striker Clive) opened the scoring after 15 minutes. A 1-0 score line at halftime followed by a goal by Derek Gibbs gave the Blues a 2-0 victory. The second half was shown live on ITV. Almost 30 years after their first ever game under floodlights the crowd were entertained by the idea of a midweek evening atmosphere and this led to the introduction of the football league cup in the 1960/61 season.

GAME 27
Flying home

Newcastle 1 Chelsea 2
19th April 1957

Football League Division One
St James' Park
Chelsea; Reg Matthews, Richard Whittaker, Peter Sillett, Brian Nicholas, Alan Dicks, Derek Saunders, Peter Brabrook, Ron Tindall, Les Allen, Les Stubbs, Jim Lewis
Scorers; Stubbs, Saunders
Manager; Ted Drake
Referee; Arthur Luty
Attendance; 32,000

In the bygone years of football many players would travel to games by train, often accompanied by team supporters filling the same carriages. Nowadays teams travel in more luxurious ways and rarely come into contact with fans. This is a part of the game that older fans feel has been lost over the years as these professionals become more untouchable than ever.

Back in 1957 Chelsea played Newcastle at St James' Park and won 2-1 courtesy of goals from Les Stubbs and Derek Saunders. Len White did score for the Geordies but it wasn't enough. There wasn't enough time for the Blues to recover before their next match, less than 24 hours away against Everton at Stamford Bridge.

The club thought that a 280 mile round trip back to London would be too much for the players to take and so, out of necessity rather than extravagance, hired a private jet to take them back to the capital. This was the first time in English history that a team had travelled by plane from a domestic football match. The idea proved to be successful as Chelsea beat the Merseysiders 5-1.

So, in a world where footballers are like celebrities and live a life of luxury it was Ted Drake's Chelsea team back in 1957 that started the jet-set life.

GAME 28
First European game

Frem Copenhagen 1 Chelsea 3
30th September 1958

Fairs Cup Round 1 (1st leg)

Valby Idraetspark

Chelsea; Reg Matthews, Peter Sillett, John Sillett, Cliff Huxford, Mel Scott, Derek Saunders, Colin Court, Jimmy Greaves, Ron Tindall, Tony Nicholas, Mike Harrison

Scorers; Harrison, Greaves, Nicholas

Manager; Ted Drake

Referee; Pierre Schwinte

Attendance; 19,200

Up until the 1950s the closest English teams came to continental football were trips to Wales or pre-season friendlies overseas. In 1955 the European Cup was formed which consisted of the champions of each European country that entered the competition. However, there was another competition also making its way into European football.

The Inter Cities Fairs Cup was the idea of a few men who later went on to be senior officials of FIFA. The competition was set up for teams that were hosting trade fairs to officially compete. This meant that the finishing position in the league had no bearing on qualification although this did change in the late 1960s.

The initial tournament was spread out over three years from 1955 to 1958. A London XI was entered, managed by Chelsea chairman Joe Mears. He took the side to the final which was a two-legged affair. The first leg was played at Stamford Bridge and ended in a 2-2 draw with Jimmy Greaves scoring one of the goals. However, in the second leg it was Barcelona who dominated the game and won 6-0.

In 1958 the new tournament started all over again except there were two representatives from England. They were Birmingham City and Chelsea. This time Ted Drake was the Chelsea manager and so he took charge of the team rather than Mears. In the first round the Blues were paired with Frem Copenhagen.

On the 30th of September 1958 Drake took his side to Denmark to play in front of a crowd of nearly 20,000. This was Chelsea's first ever game in European competition. Mike Harrison opened the scoring and with that became the club's first ever goalscorer in European competition. The lead only lasted two minutes when Harald Gronemann equalised. In the second half goals from Jimmy Greaves and Tony Nicholas gave the Blues a 3-1 advantage heading back to Stamford Bridge in November. Chelsea won that game 4-1. They did however lose in the next round to Red Star Belgrade despite winning the first leg.

GAME 29
Greaves' goodbye gift

Chelsea 4 Nottingham Forest 3
29th April 1961

Football League Division One
Stamford Bridge
Chelsea; Peter Bonetti, John Sillett, Allan Harris, Terry Venables, Mel Scott, Sylvan Anderton, Peter Brabrook, Jimmy Greaves, Ron Tindall, Bobby Tambling, Frank Blunstone
Scorer; Greaves (4)
Manager; Ted Drake
Referee; JS Pickles
Attendance; 22,775

In 2010 the Chelsea youth team won the FA Youth Cup for the first time since 1961. After that they went on to win the trophy again in 2012 and then five consecutive finals from 2014 to 2018. The club had one of the most talked about youth set ups in the world. But, despite all the team success, there were many people concerned that none of the players were good enough or given a chance. The last great youth team player to make a name for himself was John Terry and he made his debut in 1998.

However, back in the 1950s the Blues relied on their youth team to provide players for the first team. Legends such as Peter Bonetti, Ron Harris, Bobby Tambling, Ray Wilkins and Peter Osgood played for the juniors. However, there was one player who would go on to become a goal scoring machine at both club and international level.

Jimmy Greaves was spotted as a 15 year old and signed for Chelsea as an apprentice to become one of Drake's Ducklings. In the 1955-56 season he netted a total of 51 goals at youth level. A year later he had managed to score over 100 more in Dickie Foss' youth team. His goal scoring exploits caught the eye of the first team manager, Ted Drake.

Greaves was given his debut on the opening day of the 1957-58 season. Chelsea took on Tottenham at Stamford Bridge and earned a 1-1 draw. It was the young striker who scored for the Blues on his debut at the age of 17 years and 186 days. The press had hailed his performance and it was clear that big things were in store for Greaves.

By the time of his twentieth birthday his goal tally stood at 82 and scored his 100th goal against Blackpool at the age of 20 years and 217 days. During his time at Chelsea he managed to score 132 goals in just 169 games, including 13 hat tricks. In 1961, at the age of 21, he signed for Italian giants AC Milan for a fee of £80,000.

Chairman Joe Mears had agreed to sell Greaves before the end of the season and the Blues were able to show their appreciation of their talisman by making him captain in his final game. On the 29th of April 1961 Greaves took the armband against Nottingham Forest. It was a day of mixed emotions for fans and player alike. The young striker didn't really want to leave but the club needed the money.

Chelsea took the lead in the first half through none other than Jimmy Greaves. In fact he made it 2-0 before half time. Forest got a goal back early in the second half but Greaves bagged his hattrick ten minutes later. The visitors did score twice more and the game was level at 3-3. The game looked as though it would end in a draw until the referee pointed to the spot as he awarded Chelsea a penalty. Up stepped Greaves and he shot past Peter Grummitt to give his side a 4-3 win. His parting gift to the club was four goals in his final game to ensure his team won.

Jimmy Greaves made his England debut whilst at Chelsea and after he left

AC Milan he joined Tottenham even though he was offered back to the Blues. In total the former youth team star scored 357 top flight goals and a further 44 for England. He was part of England's World Cup winning squad and would likely to have played in the final if not for being studded in the leg by France's Joseph Bonnel which resulted in 14 stitches, a permanent scar and no further part in the tournament. His place was taken by Geoff Hurst who famously scored a hattrick as England beat West Germany in the final. Greaves also holds the record for most England hat tricks with a total of six.

GAME 30
Back to the First Division

Chelsea 7 Portsmouth 0
21st May 1963

Football League Division Two
Stamford Bridge
Chelsea; Peter Bonetti, Ken Shellito, Eddie McCreadie, Terry Venables, John Mortimore, Ron Harris, Frank Blunstone, Derek Kevan, Frank Upton, Tommy Harmer, Bobby Tambling
Scorers; Tambling (4), Kevan, Blunstone, Venables
Manager; Tommy Docherty
Referee; Ray Aldous
Attendance; 54,558

Despite winning the league in 1955 Chelsea found themselves relegated just seven years later, finishing bottom of the First Division. There were a few changes during that season including Ted Drake being replaced by Tommy Docherty as the Blues boss in October 1961. 'The Doc' was unable to avoid relegation but was kept on for the following season.

Chelsea had mounted a serious promotion campaign in 1962 and were sitting top of the division from the end of October until March. The Blues stayed in the top two until May. With only three games to go they faced table toppers Stoke City at Stamford Bridge. A 1-0 defeat saw them slump to third and out of the promotion places

Next up Chelsea had to play Sunderland at Roker Park in front of a crowd of nearly 48,000. A win for the Mackems would see them join Stoke enjoying the next season back in England's top flight. However, it was a better result for the Blues as Tommy Harmer's first half goal ensured that the final game of the season would go down to the wire. This was the Black Cat's last match and they eagerly awaited to see how the Blues would get on.

On Tuesday 21st May 1963 Chelsea took on a Portsmouth side at Stamford Bridge. Only a win for the home side would do. They knew they already had a better goal average than Sunderland so even a 1-0 win would have been enough to seal promotion.

The game couldn't have started any better for Chelsea as a crowd of 54,558 saw Derek Kevan score after just two minutes in his final appearance. Bobby Tambling made it 3-0 after scoring a brace after half an hour. Nowadays most teams would sit on this kind of lead with only 45 minutes to go but the Blues wanted to go up in style. A Terry Venables penalty and a goal from Frank Blunstone were sandwiched between another two from Bobby Tambling, taking his goal tally to four in the game and 35 for the season. This ensured that Tambling finished the top goalscorer in the division. The clean sheet also meant that Chelsea had the meanest defence, only shipping in 42 goals. The boys in Blue from Division Two weren't there for long!

GAME 31
New club colours

Chelsea 2 Aston Villa 1
26th August 1964

Football League Division One
Stamford Bridge
Chelsea; Peter Bonetti, Ken Shellito, Eddie McCreadie, John Hollins, Marvin Hinton, Ron Harris, Bert Murray, Bobby Tambling, Barry Bridges, Terry Venables, Tommy Knox
Scorers; Tambling, Bridges
Manager; Tommy Docherty
Referee; Harry G New
Attendance; 30,389

Tommy Docherty was putting together a Chelsea side that the fans could be proud of. The season after being promoted in 1963 they fought hard in England's top flight. Although they hovered around mid-table for most of the season a late charge saw them finish 3rd, their second highest ever finishing position.

It wasn't just form and league positions that were changing at the club. On the 26th of August 1964 Chelsea entered the pitch wearing a new look kit. The team wore royal blue shirts and shorts along with white socks, which are now the club's official club colours. Previously white shorts had been worn and sock colours varied over time.

The new kit for the first home game of the campaign proved to be successful as the home side won 2-1 with goals from Bobby Tambling and Barry Bridges before future Chelsea striker Tony Hateley netted a consolation goal for the Villans.

65

GAME 32
First major cup win

Leicester 0 Chelsea 0
5th April 1965

League Cup Final (2nd leg)
Filbert Street
Chelsea; Peter Bonetti, Marvin Hinton, Eddie McCreadie, Ron Harris, John Mortimore, Frank Upton, Bert Murray, John Boyle, Barry Bridges, Terry Venables, Bobby Tambling
Manager; Tommy Docherty
Referee; Kevin Howley
Attendance; 26,957

Chelsea had won the league a decade earlier but in their 60 year history they had only ever been in one cup final, a 3-0 loss to Sheffield Utd in 1915. The introduction of the League Cup in 1960 allowed more teams to taste success on a domestic front. Despite objections from some clubs the new cup format was started and continues to this very day.

The Blues lost 1-0 in the fourth round to Portsmouth despite beating Millwall (7-1), Workington (4-2) and Doncaster Rovers (7-0). However, the competition was not compulsory and Chelsea did not enter for the following two seasons.

In the 1964/65 season Chelsea were battling hard on all fronts. They would finish the league in third place and reach an FA Cup semi final but it was the League Cup that brought more success. The Blues had managed to beat Aston Villa in the semi final and only a two-legged final vs Leicester stood in their way of their first ever trophy in cup competition.

On the 15th of March Chelsea entertained the Foxes at Stamford Bridge in front of a crowd over 20,000. Bobby Tambling gave the home side a 1-0 lead but Colin Appleton equalised early in the second half. A Terry Venables penalty put Chelsea back in front until Jimmy Goodfellow levelled things up with fifteen minutes to go. However, Eddie McCreadie's late goal gave his side a 3-2 advantage to take into the second leg at Filbert Street a few weeks later.

The second leg of the 1964/65 League Cup final was not full of goals like the first leg. A goalless draw was enough though for Chelsea to celebrate winning their first ever domestic cup success. Tommy Docherty's men were looking like one of the strongest sides in English football.

GAME 33
The first substitute

Fulham 0 Chelsea 3
28th August 1965

Football League Division One
Craven Cottage
Chelsea; Peter Bonetti, Ken Shellito, Eddie McCreadie, John Hollins, Marvin Hinton, Ron Harris, Bert Murray, George Graham (John Boyle 80), Barry Bridges, Terry Venables, Bobby Tambling
Scorers; Murray, Bridges, Graham
Manager; Tommy Docherty
Referee; Jack K Taylor
Attendance; 34,027

A radical new change happened in English football in 1965, the introduction of substitutions. Teams could name one sub and they were only allowed to replace injured players. It wasn't until a couple of years later that substitutions could be made for tactical reasons.

The first game of the season saw Chelsea take on Burnley at Stamford Bridge. The game ended 1-1 with goals from Terry Venables and Arthur Bellamy. It was Bert Murray who was named as Chelsea's substitute for the game but because there were no injuries he was not permitted to play.

One week later the Blues travelled the short distance to West London neighbours Fulham. It was Chelsea who looked like they were at home after entering the half time interval, leading 3-0 with goals from Bert Murray, Barry Bridges and George Graham. Fulham did make a change at half time when Graham Leggat replaced Johnny Haynes. However, with ten minutes to go, an injury to scorer George Graham meant it was time for Chelsea to make their first ever substitution. Johnny Boyle came on to replace Graham and helped the visitors keep their 3-0 lead and a win over Fulham.

It wasn't until the following season that Peter Houseman became the club's first ever super sub after scoring against Charlton in a 5-2 win after he replaced Peter Osgood.

GAME 34
Heads or tails

AC Milan 1 Chelsea 1
(After extra time. Won on toss of coin)
2nd March 1966

UEFA Cup Round 3 (Playoff)

San Siro

Chelsea; Peter Bonetti, Ron Harris, Eddie McCreadie, John Hollins, Marvin Hinton, John Boyle, Barry Bridges, George Graham, Peter Osgood, Bert Murray, Bobby Tambling

Scorer; Bridges

Booked; Bridges

Manager; Tommy Docherty

Referee; H Baumgartner

Attendance; 40,000

Chelsea had already taken part in European competition back in 1958 when they reached the second round of the Inter-Cities Fairs Cup. The Blues entered the same competition in 1965 and saw themselves drawn against Roma in the first round. It was Chelsea who won the first leg 4-1 before securing a 0-0 draw away to progress into the next round.

In the second round Chelsea were paired against Wiener from Austria. A crowd of 4,000 saw the Austrian side win 1-0 courtesy of a Wolfgang Gayer penalty in the 85th minute. Marvin Hinton was sent off for the Blues just five minutes earlier. The return leg was played at Stamford Bridge two weeks later. Despite his sending off in the first leg Marvin Hinton was available for selection and played all 90 minutes. An improved crowd of over 28,000 attended the game, which was lower than the average league attendance. The loyal fans didn't have to wait long for something to cheer about as Bert

Murray put the Blues ahead and Peter Osgood's goal after half an hour was the final goal of the game, sealing a 2-1 aggregate win and a next round tie against AC Milan.

Similar to the previous round the Blues were drawn away first and ended up on the wrong side of a 2-1 defeat at the San Siro. Milan took a 2-0 lead and missed a penalty before a late consolation goal from George Graham gave Chelsea hope for the return leg. A week later the tables turned and it was the Blues who tasted victory by the same scoreline. Graham again netted first and Peter Osgood added another to give the home side a 2-0 lead after just 20 minutes. The Italians did get a goal back just before half time to make the score 3-3 on aggregate. When the final whistle blew the referee gathered the two captains for a coin toss. AC Milan won the toss and were able to choose a venue for the play-off game. Unsurprisingly they chose the San Siro again.

A crowd of 40,000 came to the game. This was a huge improvement from the 11,000 or so from the first leg. However, it was the travelling fans enjoying most of the game as Barry Bridges gave them a 1-0 advantage before the break. As the game drew closer to a finish the Italians snatched a last minute goal and thus sending the game into extra time. The following 30 minutes produced no other goals and so the referee gathered both captains together again. This time the winner of the coin toss would determine who would progress in the competition. Luckily for Chelsea, captain Ron Harris guessed correctly and the Blues won the tie on the toss of a coin.

GAME 35
Beam back

Barcelona 5 Chelsea 0
25th May 1966

UEFA Cup Round Semi-Final (Playoff)
Nou Camp
Chelsea; Peter Bonetti, Joe Kirkup, Allan Harris, John Hollins, Marvin Hinton, Ron Harris, John Boyle, George Graham, Peter Osgood, Charlie Cooke, Bobby Tambling
Manager; Tommy Docherty
Referee; Kurt Tschenscher
Attendance; 40,000

Chelsea were enjoying their travels across Europe in the Inter-Cities Fairs Cup. They had already beaten off competition from Roma, AC Milan and 1860 Munich. The win over the German team set up a tie against Barcelona in the semi finals. The winner would take on Real Zaragoza from Spain in the final.

Things did not start well for Chelsea. The Blues saw themselves losing 2-0 by the end of the first leg courtesy of goals from Jose Maria Fuste and Jose Antonio Zaldua. This would also be Terry Venables final appearance for Chelsea before he made his move to North London rivals Tottenham. Venables would later go on to manage both Spurs and Barcelona in the future.

The return leg proved to be much better for Chelsea. A sending off for Barcelona's Silvestre Eladio after 40 minutes meant they had to play the rest of the game with ten men. However, it may have seemed like the team from Catalonia had a few less players as Francisco Gallego scored an own goal with 20 minutes to play. In a bizzare twist of fate Chelsea scored again, or rather it was another own goal by Miguel Reina to make the score 2-2 on aggregate. At the end of the game Barcelona won the coin toss and decided the play-off game be played back at the Nou Camp.

Sadly, this was to be the end of the road for Chelsea as they were thrashed 5-0. However, this game will go down in history as the first European match transmitted back to England and shown live on closed circuit TV. Now football is broadcast all over the world in many formats but perhaps this was the start of the football being watched live by fans all over the world.

GAME 36
The youngest debut and goalscorer

Tottenham 1 Chelsea 1
18th March 1967

Football League Division One
White Hart Lane
Chelsea; Peter Bonetti, Allan Harris, Eddie McCreadie, John Hollins, Marvin Hinton, Ron Harris, John Boyle, Tommy Baldwin, Tony Hateley, Ian Hamilton, Jim Thomson
Scorer; Hamilton
Manager; Tommy Docherty
Referee; Peter Walters
Attendance; 49,553

Long before foreign owners came to buy up English football clubs, teams would rely on local talent including the use of their own academy and youth systems. The FA Youth Cup was set up in 1952 and Chelsea were winners in both 1960 and 1961. They boasted future stars and legends such as Peter Bonetti, Ron Harris, Terry Venables, Bert Murry and Bobby Tambling.

Jimmy Greaves had come through the Blues youth set up and scored 132 goals in just 169 games before moving to AC Milan for £80,000 in 1961. Less than a year later he moved back to England with Spurs prepared to pay his £99,999 transfer fee. He made his Chelsea debut in 1957 in a 1-1 draw at White Hart Lane. The young Englishmen scored on his debut at the age of 17 years and 186 days. This made him the youngest ever person to score on his Blues debut.

In the 1966/67 season Chelsea were mounting a good run in the FA Cup and even managed to make it to the final. However, it was a league game on the 18th March that created history for the Blues as they took a trip to Tottenham and played out a 1-1 draw. Almost ten years after his CFC debut Jimmy Greaves was playing for Spurs and actually netted after just ten minutes. Things were looking good for Tottenham until there were twenty minutes left on the clock.

Chelsea had given a debut to Ian 'Chico' Hamilton, a young English midfielder from Streatham. At the age of 16 years and 138 days he became the Blues youngest ever player. Things got even better for Chico when he scored past the highly rated Northern Ireland goalkeeper Pat Jennings. This made him the youngest person to ever score for Chelsea as well. Hamilton only played five times for the first team, scoring two goals, before moving on to Southend, Aston Villa, Sheffield Utd and a stint in North America.

GAME 37
Tambling scored his 200th goal

Chelsea 2 Coventry 1
10th March 1969

Football League Division One
Stamford Bridge
Chelsea; Peter Bonetti, David Webb, Eddie McCreadie, John Hollins, John Dempsey, Ron Harris, John Boyle, Bobby Tambling, Ian Hutchinson, Alan Birchenall, Peter Houseman
Scorers; Hutchinson, Tambling
Manager; Dave Sexton
Referee; Ray Tinkler
Attendance; 17,639

The 1968/69 season was the first time that Chelsea had competed in four different competitions. Their results in cup games meant they did not get near any silverware but did try to mount a more serious push for the league title.

Bobby Tambling was looking to build on his impressive goal tally for the Blues. He was already the club's highest ever goalscorer but was hunting down a landmark of his own. He began the season on 183 goals for Chelsea and another typical Tambling season should have seen him reach the 200 goal landmark.

On the 22nd of February 1969 Chelsea entertained Sunderland at Stamford Bridge. The Blues won comfortably with a 5-1 score line thanks mainly to Bobby Tambling who netted four times in the second half. The fourth goal of the game was Tambling's 199th in a Chelsea shirt. In the next three games his side beat Stoke, lost to West Brom in the FA Cup but got their revenge with a 3-0 win in the league. After these matches Bobby Tambling's goal tally remained on 199.

On the 10th of March 1969, exactly 64 years after Chelsea were formed, a Coventry side visited Stamford Bridge for a Monday night kick off. The Sky Blues were caught in a relegation battle and needed every point they could get. However, this idea was cut short when Ian Hutchinson scored after just two minutes. Another twenty minutes went past and the ball fell to Tambling who scored against Coventry's keeper Bill Glazier. Finally the Blues striker and youth team product scored his all important 200th goal for the club becoming the first ever player in Chelsea history to reach the landmark. Amazingly Bobby Tambling only went on to score another two goals in a Blues shirt before moving Crystal Palace in 1970 at the age of 28.

GAME 38
FA Cup triumph

Chelsea 2 Leeds 1
(After extra time. Score at 90 minutes 1-1)
29th April 1970

FA Cup Final (Replay)
Old Trafford
Chelsea; Peter Bonetti, Ron Harris, Eddie McCreadie, John Hollins, John Dempsey, David Webb, Tommy Baldwin, Charlie Cooke, Peter Osgood (Marvin Hinton 112), Ian Hutchinson, Peter Houseman
Scorers; Osgood, Webb
Manager; Dave Sexton
Referee; Eric T Jennings
Attendance; 62,078

In 1970 Chelsea reached the FA Cup final for the third time in their history. Their cup run started at home to Birmingham City with a comfortable 3-0 win courtesy of goals from Ian Hutchinson (2) and Peter Osgood. In the fourth round the Blues welcomed Burnley to Stamford Bridge. Chelsea looked to be cruising into the next round when goals from John Hollins put them 2-0 up with twenty minutes to go. However the visitors had other plans and Martin Dobson scored twice in the last ten minutes to force a replay. The game at Turf Moor needed to be settled in extra time. Ralph Coates scored Burnley's goal but Peter Houseman equalised. Further goals from Tommy Baldwin and Houseman again meant Chelsea would meet London rivals Crystal Palace in the fifth round.

The Blues beat Palace comfortably in a 4-1 victory which saw Osgood, John Dempsey, Houseman and Hutchinson get the goals. It was the same result in the quarter finals against West London neighbours QPR where they scored another four goals from Webb and Osgood (3) although former Blues Terry Venables (penalty) and Barry Bridges scored for the hoops.

Next up a semi final vs Watford at White Hart Lane. A trip to Wembley was only a win away and things started well when Webb scored after three minutes. Watford did equalise through Terry Garbett to make the score 1-1 at half time. Whatever Chelsea manager Dave Sexton said at half time certainly worked as the Blues scored four more goals, Osgood, Houseman (2) and Hutchinson getting the goals. Their reward for a 5-1 victory was a trip to Wembley in the FA Cup final against title rivals Leeds Utd. An injury to Chelsea's young midfield maestro Alan Hudson less than two weeks before the final meant he would miss his opportunity to play in the big game.

Wembley was the showpiece of world football, however for the 1970 FA Cup final the pitch did not match that image. The ground had held the Horse of the Year show just days earlier and the pitch had been heavily sanded. Leeds were marginal favourites for the win and on the day performed as such, especially when they took the lead after 21 minutes. Peter Houseman got a goal back courtesy of an error by Leeds' goalkeeper, Gary Sprake. With less than ten minutes to go Mick Jones scored with his left foot but the determination of Chelsea did not disappear and a late header from Ian Hutchinson sent the tie to a replay, which would be played at Old Trafford.

There was an 18 day wait between the final and the replay. Leeds had finished two points, and one place, above Chelsea in the league. Mick Jones put Leeds in front after 36 minutes but a header from Peter Osgood sent the game into extra time. This goal was historic for Osgood as he had scored in all the other rounds that season. Just at the end of the first half of extra time Chelsea had a throw in. The long throw by Ian Hutchinson, known as the windmill, entered into the box. The ball was flicked on by Leeds' Jack Charlton and David Webb was on hand to bundle the goal in. This was the first time the Blues had taken a lead in the tie. Chelsea kept the score at 2-1 and Bonetti, Harris, Ossie and co lifted the FA Cup for the first time in their history.

This game will go down in Chelsea history for the trophy but will be remembered by others as the dirtiest ever FA Cup final. Also, 28.49m people tuned in to the FA Cup Final replay making it the fourth highest ever TV audience figure.

GAME 39
The fastest goal

Chelsea 3 Middlesbrough 2
7th October 1970

League Cup Round 3
Stamford Bridge
Chelsea; Peter Bonetti, John Boyle (Stewart Houston), Ron Harris, John Hollins, Marvin Hinton, David Webb, Keith Weller, Charlie Cooke, Tommy Baldwin, Ian Hutchinson, Peter Houseman
Scorers; Weller, Baldwin, Hutchinson
Manager; Dave Sexton
Referee; John Hunting
Attendance; 28,597

Chelsea took on Middlesbrough at Stamford Bridge in the League Cup third round. The Blues were looking to get back to winning ways after losing 1-0 away at Liverpool. This looked like just the right fixture for Chelsea as Middlesbrough were playing in the division below.

At 19:30 referee John Hunting blew his whistle to start the game. Within 12 seconds the Blues winger, Keith Weller, had received the ball, pushed it past 'Boro fullback Gordon Jones and scored. This was the quickest recorded goal in CFC history. Things got even better when Tommy Baldwin headed in a corner from Charlie Cooke after just three minutes. Ian Hutchinson made it 3-0 after 13 minutes and were cruising to victory.

It wasn't until near the end of 90 minutes that Middlesbrough mounted any real threat. With just three minutes to play John Hickton got a goal back for the visitors. The Chelsea fans were looking a bit nervous when 'Boro scored again in the 90th minute but it wasn't enough and Chelsea went through to play Man Utd in the next round.

GAME 40
The first European trophy

Chelsea 2 Real Madrid 1
21st May 1971

UEFA Cup Winners Cup Final (Replay)
Karaiskaki Stadium
Chelsea; Peter Bonetti, John Boyle, Ron Harris, Charlie Cooke, John Dempsey, David Webb, Keith Weller, Tommy Baldwin, Peter Osgood (Derek Smethurst 75), Alan Hudson, Peter Houseman
Scorers; Dempsey, Osgood
Manager; Dave Sexton
Referee; Anton Buchelli
Attendance; 24,000

As Chelsea had won the FA Cup they were given the chance to compete in the European Cup Winners Cup the following season. However, the Blues were not the only representatives from England as Man City had won the competition the previous year and were allowed to defend their trophy.

In the first round Chelsea were paired with Aris Salonika from Greece. The first leg ended 1-1 although was not short of drama. The Blues were awarded a penalty around the half hour mark when Christos Nalbantis brought down Paddy Mulligan but Peter Osgood had his spot kick saved by Nicolas Christidis. The Blues were reduced to ten men when John Dempsey was sent off after 36 minutes. Salonika took the lead through Alecos Alexiadis but Ian Hutchinson equalised for the visitors. The second leg was a much more comfortable result as Chelsea won 5-1 with an aggregate score of 6-2.

The next two rounds saw the Blues beat CSKA Sofia (2-0) and Brugge (4-2) to set up a semi final tie against the current holders Manchester City. They had already drawn 1-1 in a league game back in October. Also, Man City had knocked Chelsea out of the FA Cup after winning 3-0 at the Bridge. Another league game between the two sides was set to be played inbetween the two European legs.

The first leg was played at Stamford Bridge and the only difference between the two teams was a single goal from Derek Smethurst early in the second half. Three days later the two teams played out a 1-1 draw in the league. Things were tight in the second leg, again with a 1-0 scoreline. It was Manchester City's Ron Healey who scored the only goal of the game. Unfortunately for him it was in his own net from a Chelsea corner. A 2-0 aggregate win would set up a return to Greece for the final, except this time they would face European giants Real Madrid.

4,000 Chelsea fans travelled to Athens to watch the Blues in their first ever European final. Peter Osgood scored a left footed volley from inside the area to send the English fans into a frenzy. No matter what Real Madrid threw at Chelsea they were unable to break down their defence. Towards the end of the game the trophy was carried to the touchline waiting for captain Ron Harris and his team mates to collect it. However, in the 90th minute John Dempsey miskicked the ball and Spanish midfielder Ignacio Zoco scored to send the game into extra time. The linesman did raise his flag but it was ignored by referee Rudolf Scheurer from Switzerland. After an additional 30 minutes the score remained the same meaning the two teams would need to meet in a replay just two days later.

Many Chelsea supporters had already travelled home by the time the replay took place. A crowd of 20,000 attended the match compared to 45,000 just days before. John Hollins had collected an injury and would be forced out of the replay. Peter Osgood was then put into midfield as his replacement and Tommy Baldwin was recalled into the Blues frontline.

John Dempsey was looking to make amends for his error in the previous game and he certainly did when his 32nd minute volley almost broke the net. It was less than ten minutes later when Osgood scored to double Chelsea's lead. Things were looking good for the Blues. Real Madrid did manage to score a consolation goal with quarter of an hour to go but it was not enough and Dave Sexton's men were crowned the European Cup Winners Cup winners.

GAME 41
A record win

Chelsea 13 Jeunesse Hautcharage 0
29th September 1971

UEFA Cup Winners Cup Round 1 (2nd Leg)
Stamford Bridge
Chelsea; Peter Bonetti, John Boyle, Ron Harris, John Hollins, David Webb, Marvin Hinton, Charlie Cooke, Tommy Baldwin, Peter Osgood, Alan Hudson, Peter Houseman
Scorers; Osgood (5), Baldwin (3), Hudson, Hollins, Houseman, Harris, Webb
Manager; Dave Sexton
Referee; Richard Navarra
Attendance; 27,621

Chelsea were one of the favourites to win the European Cup Winners Cup in the 1971/72 season as they managed to beat Real Madrid in the final the previous season. Arsenal beat Liverpool in the FA Cup final and so, again, there were two English sides aiming to win the trophy.

The Blues were handed an easy first round tie against European minnows Jeunesse Hautcharage from Luxembourg. The team were amateurs and had day jobs including steelworkers, hairdresser, station master and butcher. In addition they had a one armed striker, a midfielder who wore glasses and there were four brothers who all played in the game. The first leg was played in Luxembourg and a crowd of 13,000 came to watch the game, much higher than the average attendance of 700.

The Londoners showed their muscle and gained an 8-0 victory to take back to Stamford Bridge. Peter Osgood (3), Peter Houseman (2), John Hollins, Tommy Baldwin and David Webb got the goals. There was one unfortunate event as defender John Dempsey received a head injury requiring two stitches and so Marvin Hinton replaced him at half time.

Two weeks later the return game was played at Stamford Bridge. The Blues were looking to beat the European goalscoring record set by Benfica when they beat Stade Dudelange 18–0 in the preliminary round of the European Cup in 1965–66.

All eyes were on how many goals Chelsea would score. Peter Osgood set his sights on improving his three goal tally from the first leg. At the end of 90 minutes the Blues had won 13-0 with goals from Osgood (5), Baldwin (3), Houseman, Hudson, Webb, Hollins and Ron Harris. The visitors did bring on a 15 year old schoolboy as a sub.

Chelsea's 21-0 aggregate score was a new European record for the biggest ever two-legged aggregate win. The plaudits didn't last long as surprisingly the Blues were knocked out of the competition in the next round on the away goals rule when Swedish part-timers Atvidaberg drew 1-1 at Stamford Bridge following a goalless draw at Kopparvallen.

GAME 42
A man for all positions

Chelsea 2 Ipswich 0
27th December 1971

Football League Division One
Stamford Bridge
Chelsea; David Webb, Ron Harris, Peter Houseman, John Hollins, John Dempsey, Paddy Mulligan, Chris Garland, Steve Kember, Peter Osgood, Alan Hudson, Tommy Baldwin (Charlie Cooke 56)
Scorers; Kember, Garland
Manager; Dave Sexton
Referee; Anthony P Oliver
Attendance; 43,896

It was the festive season and everyone was in good cheer. Chelsea had only lost one league game since the end of September despite sitting in mid table. Ipswich were the visitors to Stamford Bridge and were winless against the Blues in the previous nine league meetings.

Chelsea goalkeeper Peter Bonetti was unavailable through injury so reserve keeper John Phillips was set to take his place. However a late injury to the Welshman meant that manager Dave Sexton had to call the third choice shot stopper, Steve Sherwood. As it was Christmas time Sherwod had gone to stay with his family in Yorkshire. He dashed down the motorway as soon as he got the call but did not arrive at the ground until three minutes before kick off, ruling him out of the match.

As Chelsea had no goalkeeper available they relied on one of the outfield players to go in goal. Up stepped David Webb who agreed to put on the green shirt and gloves. Webb was called upon in the sixth minute and his heroics resulted in a corner for Ipswich. The crowd cheered every time the utility man touched the ball and the score was goalless at half time.

Steve Kember put Chelsea ahead in the 65th minute following Paddy Mulligan's flick on from a Charlie Cooke corner. Chris Garland doubled their lead ten minutes later after some skillful play from Peter Osgood. The Blues won 2-0 with David Webb keeping a clean sheet. However, it was Sherwood who was called upon for the next game where Chelsea lost 1-0 to Derby. The only goal of the game was an own goal scored by... David Webb!

GAME 43
Super Sunday

Stoke 1 Chelsea 0
27th January 1974

Football League Division One
Victoria Ground
Chelsea; John Phillips, Gary Locke, Ron Harris, John Hollins, Micky Droy, David Webb, Ian Britton, Chris Garland, Steve Kember, Bill Garner, Charlie Cooke
Manager; Dave Sexton
Referee; Ivan T Smith
Attendance; 31,985

In 1973 the Yom Kippur war was going on which meant that many Arab countries suspended deliveries of oil to Western nations, including England. A state of emergency was declared and the idea of a 'three day week' was introduced to save electricity. The use of floodlights at football grounds were banned so all matches had to be played during the day time. Some clubs wanted to postpone matches at the end of the season due to a potential fixture chaos especially as proposals to extend the league to end in June were rejected.

By the end of 1973 the FA asked for permission to stage football matches on a Sunday. This change was not universally popular but was accepted. There were huge factors to consider such as transport to and from the game as a Sunday Service was in place. The high rising cost of petrol coupled with employment uncertainty meant many people just couldn't afford to watch their team play.

Some people, including players, refused to take part in Sunday games due to religious observance. This was not the main obstacle to Sunday football though, that was down to the law. The Sunday Observance Act (1780) forbid admission charges for football matches (and other events). However, clubs got around this by giving free entry to all supporters as long as they bought a programme at the turnstile.

Chelsea took on Stoke City at the Victoria Ground. This was the first ever First Division match played on a Sunday (excluding public holidays). World Cup hero and future Blues manager Geoff Hurst scored the only goal of the game via the penalty spot. For most football fans it's hard to imagine that watching football on a Sunday would be quite as controversial as it was, especially now that you can almost guarantee a minimum of three televised games every Sunday. How times have changed!

GAME 44
'Urry up, it's only a pound

Chelsea 1 Millwall 1
12th February 1977

Football League Division Two
Stamford Bridge
Chelsea; John Phillips, Gary Locke, Ron Harris, Garry Stanley, Micky Droy, David Hay, Ian Britton, Ray Wilkins, Teddy Maybank, Ray Lewington, Ken Swain
Scorer; Stanley
Manager; Eddie McCreadie
Referee; Derek Nippard
Attendance; 34,857

Football has always been a game for the people but in recent years the money, for some clubs, has become as important, if not more, than trophy success. The growing worldwide interest in football has contributed to the vast amounts of money being given to clubs which is then spent on player's wages and transfers. In turn costs have also been handed down to match going supporters and the high priced tickets has made the game less for 'everyone' and more for 'those that can afford it'.

At the 1972 League Cup final between Chelsea and Stoke City standing tickets were priced around 60p. However for the home game vs Millwall five years later a new price benchmark was set. This game saw the Blues charge a £1 admission for standing for the first time.

Millwall took the lead in the second half when Terry Brisley scored from a corner. Soon after Chelsea's Micky Droy collided with the visitor's keeper Ray Goddard which left the shot stopper with a badly split eyelid. He was taken off temporarily for treatment and defender Dave Donaldson went in goal. It wasn't long until Chelsea took advantage of this and Garry Stanley equalised, again from a corner.

It's hard to imagine how football clubs survived with such low admission prices but that just shows how much our hunger for more football has changed as well as the cost of supporting a team.

GAME 45
An FA Cup shock

Chelsea 4 Liverpool 2
7th January 1978

FA Cup Round 3
Stamford Bridge
Chelsea; Peter Bonetti, Graham Wilkins, John Sparrow, Ian Britton, Ron Harris, Steve Wicks, Bill Garner, Ray Lewington, Tommy Langley, Charlie Cooke (Steve Finnieston 34), Clive Walker
Scorers; Walker (2), Finnieston, Langley
Manager; Ken Shellito
Referee; Pat Partridge
Attendance; 45,449

At the end of the 1974/75 season Chelsea were relegated into the Second Division but a couple of years later gained promotion back to the top flight. Since winning the FA Cup in 1970 the best they had managed in the competition was reaching the quarter final. Maybe this would be the Blues chance to win it again.

Chelsea were given a home fixture in the FA Cup third round. Their opponents would be Liverpool who were the reigning champions of England and Europe. They had also recently won the UEFA Super Cup by beating Hamburg 7-1 on aggregate. Things did not look good for the Blues' progression in the cup.

The home side were without their captain Ray Wilkins or tall centre half Micky Droy. In a complete shock it was Chelsea who took the lead after 16 minutes. The Blues had won a throw in inside Liverpool's half. Bill Garner found Clive Walker who ran at the Liverpool defence before letting fly a left foot shot from outside the box to score past Ray Clemence who didn't even move. The Chelsea fans erupted but they would need to hold out for another 75 minutes yet. Unfortunately for the Blues, Charlie Cooke limped off with a pulled muscle but was replaced by Steve Finneston just after the half hour mark.

At half time the score remained 1-0. Ken Shellito's young Chelsea side had done well and the manager must have been pleased with what he'd seen. Unbelievably, ten minutes into the second half the Blues had an incredible 3-0 lead courtesy of goals from substitute Finneston and Tommy Langley. Liverpool's David Johnson did get a goal back before Walker doubled his tally making it 4-1. Kenny Dalglish headed a consolation goal past Peter Bonetti but that wasn't enough to stop the home team. Chelsea had beaten the champions of Europe 4-2!

The Liverpool manager Bob Paisley described his team's performance as pathetic and the feeblest he'd seen since their relegation 24 years earlier. Chelsea, however, thrashed Burnley 6-2 in the fourth round but were knocked out by Division Two side Orient, losing 2-1 in a replay at Stamford Bridge.

GAME 46
A late comeback

Chelsea 4 Bolton 3
14th October 1978

Football League Division One
Stamford Bridge

Chelsea; Bob Iles, David Hay, David Stride, Ray Lewington, Steve Wicks, Ron Harris, Ken Swain, Ray Wilkins, Tommy Langley, Ian Britton, Garry Stanley (Clive Walker 71)

Scorers; Langley, Swain, Walker, Allardyce (O.G)

Booked; Harris

Manager; Ken Shellito

Referee; Eric A Read

Attendance; 19,879

Ask any Chelsea fan of a certain age and they will be able to tell you all about memorable comebacks. Some will point to Chelsea beating Liverpool in the 1997 FA Cup after being 2-0 down at half time. Others will talk about Spurs in 1993, Napoli, Barcelona and Bayern Munich in 2012. For those a bit older they will retell the tale of beating Bolton in 1978.

Chelsea had only won one of their opening nine games and were sitting one place above bottom placed Birmingham City. Chairman Brian Mears knew his club needed something different and so he asked former Real Madrid manager Miljan Miljanic to join his coaching staff. On the 14th of October 1978 he sat in the stands to watch the Blues take on Bolton.

The Blues had lost their last four home games and their form did not look like changing when Alan Gowling put Bolton 1-0 up after quarter of an hour. Twenty minutes later Ron Harris fouled Frank Worthington in the area and the striker converted the subsequent penalty to make it 2-0. To make matters worse Gowling got his second of the game meaning the visitors took a 3-0 scoreline into the half time interval.

Ken Shellito had told his men that it was all a matter of confidence. As the game played on Bolton appeared to relax a little and the Chelsea manager threw on Clive Walker for the last twenty minutes. His plan had an instant impact as he set up Tommy Langley a minute later. With just over five minutes left to play the Blues were on the attack and Kenny Swain scored to reduce Bolton's lead to one goal. With only three minutes on the clock it was the impressive and influential substitute Walker who went on a run and fired a shot towards goal which keeper Jim McDonagh couldn't hold onto and somehow Chelsea had rescued a point. In fact, in the dying moments of the game more pressure was piled on the Bolton defence and the unfortunate Sam Allardyce put the ball into his own net. Chelsea ran out 4-3 winners!

Miljan Miljanic was impressed by Chelsea's fighting spirit and comeback. He also watched a CFC juniors side win 5-4 that morning and was getting used to the number of goals being produced. However, Miljanic decided not to sign with Chelsea and took on the Yugoslavia manager's post for a third time. The rest of the season turned out to be terrible for the Blues. The club parted company with manager Ken Shellito in December and brought in Danny Blanchflower in hope of avoiding the drop. It didn't work as Chelsea finished bottom of the league and even went out of both domestic cups at the earliest possible opportunity.

GAME 47
The score on the board

Chelsea 1 Coventry 3
21st February 1979

Football League Division One
Stamford Bridge
Chelsea; Peter Bonetti, Graham Wilkins, David Stride, Eamonn Bannon, Ron Harris (John Sitton 46), Mike Nutton, Garry Stanley, Ray Wilkins, Trevor Aylott, Tommy Langley, Clive Walker
Scorer; Langley
Booked; G Wilkins
Manager; Danny Blanchflower
Referee; Mike J Taylor
Attendance; 15,282

Match going supporters love the atmosphere of the game which is something that you just can't get from sitting at home watching the games on TV or the internet. However, viewers at home and round the world have the advantage of seeing replays of goals and certain incidents that gives the game great talking points that allow fans to admire quality and despair in a matter of seconds. Things have become better in recent years as many clubs have electronic scoreboards that can show highlights of the game inside the ground.

On the 21st February 1979 Chelsea used an electronic scoreboard for the first time. It was very basic and could really only include text and numbers but it was still a step towards the multimedia platform in stadiums today. The Blues lost 3-1 to Coventry that day but for a short while the scoreboard read "Chelsea 1 Coventry 0. The scorer was Tommy Langley."

GAME 48
Ron Harris' last hurrah

Chelsea 3 Oldham 0
3rd May 1980

Football League Division Two
Stamford Bridge
Chelsea; Petar Borota, Gary Chivers, Dennis Rofe, John Bumstead (Micky Droy 64), Colin Pates, Mike Nutton, Ian Britton, Mike Fillery, Tommy Langley, Clive Walker, Ron Harris
Scorers; Walker (2), Fillery
Manager; Geoff Hurst
Referee; Dennis A Hedges
Attendance; 28,253

It has always been the dream of many young children to make it as a professional footballer. It is a hard road to take but the rewards can be out of this world. Some players only join a club for the money, some it's for silverware and others it's because of their love of the game in general. However, no matter what a player's motive is they all need to start somewhere.

In 1960 Allan Harris made his Chelsea debut in a League Cup match against Workington in which the Blues won 4-2. Eighteen months later it was the turn of his younger brother, Ron, to make his first Chelsea appearance in a 1-0 win vs Sheffield Wednesday. The two brothers played alongside each other as they drew 1-1 at home to Plymouth. In the end Allan played 98 games for the Blues before transferring to QPR in 1967 for £30,000.

By the time Allan had left Ron had made over 200 appearances including one as captain in an FA Cup final. He had made a name for himself and was given the nickname 'Chopper'. He stayed at the club for most of his career despite facing relegation on three separate occasions. There were times of triumph as he won the club's first ever FA Cup and European trophy in the early 1970s.

Chopper played his 500th game for the club in February 1973. He was the second person in the Blue's history to reach that landmark. The other was goalkeeper Peter Bonetti and on the 11th of March 1978 the pair of former youth team players both reached the 700 game milestone.

On the 3rd of May 1980 Chelsea took on Oldham at Stamford Bridge winning the game 3-0 with goals from Michael Fillery and a brace by Clive Walker. It would turn out to be the final game for a couple of Blues players, Tommy Langley and Ron Harris. This was the 795th game for the true Blues legend, a club record set that has not been surpassed since. His name is synonymous with both Chelsea and the 1970s football as a whole. Despite his success at club level and his longevity Harris never represented his country at first team level.

GAME 49
Bad behaviour

Chelsea 2 Tottenham 3
6th March 1982

FA Cup Round Quarter-Final
Stamford Bridge
Chelsea; Steve Francis, Gary Locke, Chris Hutchings, Mike Nutton, Gary Chivers, Colin Pates, Peter Rhoades-Brown, John Bumstead, Alan Mayes, Clive Walker (Dennis Rofe 81), Mike Fillery
Scorers; Fillery, Mayes
Manager; John Neal
Referee; George Courtney
Attendance; 42,557

The 1980's were dark days for football due to the levels of hooliganism in and around football grounds. Many fans resorted to violence against rival fans before, during and after games. Police were regularly enforced to break up horrendous behaviour amongst hooligans. However, fighting also occurred between sets of the same fans with the chance of leaving supporters badly injured or even worse. Many fans, especially those with families, were put off attending football games due to the fear of being attacked. In fact, in 1985 Chelsea youth star Robert Isaac was set to attend a match against Millwall but was attacked by a group of their fans and needed 55 stitches. It made front page news at the time.

The reputation of football fans and the game itself had a bad name. Although every club had its problems with the issue there were certain clubs that had a bigger reputation, Chelsea included. The culture of football, and society, had to change.

In 1982 Chelsea were sitting in the Second Division but had managed to put together a decent run in the FA Cup where they met Tottenham in the quarter final at Stamford Bridge. Things looked good for the Blues as they took a 1-0 lead into half time courtesy of Micky Fillery. However, Spurs went on to win 3-2 and knocked Chelsea out of the cup.

It was not the actual game that made this memorable, more the pre-match information. In an attempt to improve fan behaviour at the club Chelsea printed a special matchday programme. The front of the programme did not feature a stylish photo of the Blues in action. Rather it was just a black page with white writing with a message that warned fans that if your sole purpose is to cause trouble then you would not be welcome. If anyone was caught displaying these actions they would be ejected from the ground, banned for life and bring a private prosecution and civil claim for damages.

GAME 50
Paul Canoville makes history

Crystal Palace 0 Chelsea 1
12th April 1982

Football League Division Two
Selhurst Park
Chelsea; Steve Francis, Gary Locke, Graham Wilkins, Mike Nutton, Gary Chivers, Colin Pates, Ian Britton, Clive Walker (Paul Canoville), Colin Lee, Alan Mayes, Mike Fillery
Scorer; Walker
Manager; John Neal
Referee; Cliff Maskell
Attendance; 17,189

There are some players in Chelsea history that will go down as legends for the club for different reasons. The Kings of the Kings Road from the 1970s team alongside the heroes from the Roman Abramovich era will be remembered for the silverware they won, the style they had and their love of the club. Fans loved these players and often the feeling was reciprocated. However, this wasn't always the case.

As well as hooliganism in the 1980s, racism was also a huge problem in society. People of black and minority ethnic backgrounds were often bullied, abused and tormented. Attitudes on TV didn't help matters with the use of stereotypes feeding into people's thoughts and beliefs. The 1970s had seen the emergence of more black players featuring and starring in teams across the country. However, rival fans would often target these footballers and taunt them with racist chanting, making monkey noises and throwing bananas.

A section of the Blues fan base, like many other clubs, would even target their own fans because of the colour of their skin. But surely that wouldn't happen if a black player was playing for their team?! In 1981 Chelsea signed Paul Canoville from Hillingdon Borough for £5,000. His mother had emigrated to England from Anguilla and his dad came from Dominica.

Chelsea played London rivals Crystal Palace at Selhurst Park. The Blues were winning 1-0 courtesy of a goal from Clive Walker. Canoville was named as a sub and was asked to warm up by the manager, John Neal. As he did so, he could hear racial abuse being hurled his way. He daren't turn around but, to his surprise, he saw that the abuse was coming from his own team's fans. Canoville was then sent on as a substitute for goalscorer Walker to become the first ever black player in Chelsea history. The abuse and torment carried on for years to come but he was strong enough in character and had the support of team mates like Pat Nevin to ensure he gave his all for the club.

Without Paul Canoville there would be no Ruud Gullit. Without Gullit there would be no Desailly, Hasselbaink, Makelele, Essien, Mikel or even Didier Drogba. Paul Canoville will go down as a Chelsea legend and his story should be passed on to future Blues fans.

GAME 51
An all-English affair

Chelsea 0 Wolves 0
31st August 1982

Football League Division Two
Stamford Bridge
Chelsea; Steve Francis, Mike Nutton, Chris Hutchings, Gary Chivers, Micky Droy, Colin Pates, Clive Walker, John Bumstead, Colin Lee, Bryan Robson, Mike Fillery
Manager; John Neal
Referee; Mike J Taylor
Attendance; 14,192

In Chelsea's first ever season their squad contained players from England, Scotland and Ireland. In more recent history the Blues have had players from most European countries as well as those from around the world. For a long time all clubs were limited to the number of non-English players that could be named on the team sheet.

In December 1995 the European Court of Justice abolished the three-foreigner rule which included Scotland, Wales and Northern Ireland which were regarded as separate countries. The chief executive of the PFA at the time, Gordon Taylor, feared for the future of English football believing a flood of foreign players would be to the detriment of the game.

On the 31st August 1982 Chelsea welcomed Wolves to Stamford Bridge. The two teams played out a 0-0 draw in front of a crowd of 14,000. What makes this game special is the fact that the whole team, including Paul Canoville as an unused sub, were English. This was the last time that Chelsea fielded an all English XI and is unlikely to ever happen again.

Gordon Taylor was right about the flood of foreign players coming to England, but it's doubtful his words about them being detrimental to the game included players like Ruud Gullit, Gianfranco Zola, Didier Drogba and Eden Hazard.

GAME 52
The potential end of Chelsea

Bolton 0 Chelsea 1
7th May 1983

Football League Division Two
Burnden Park

Chelsea; Steve Francis, Joey Jones, Chris Hutchings, Gary Chivers, Micky Droy, Colin Pates, Mike Fillery, John Bumstead, Colin Lee, Paul Canoville, Clive Walker

Scorer; Walker
Manager; John Neal
Referee; Terry Holbrook
Attendance; 8,687

At the end of April 1983 Chelsea were sitting in the relegation zone by being 20th in the second division. In May the Blues managed to earn a 1-1 draw against Sheffield Wednesday who were in sixth place and looking to gain promotion. The point earned against the Owls was enough to take Chelsea out of the relegation zone by one point but the team below, Crystal Palace, had two games in hand.

Next up was an away game vs Bolton at Burnden Park. Both teams were close to being relegated. Chelsea were winless in nine games and heading towards the Third Division for the first time in their history. Financial problems also meant that relegation would certainly cripple the club and the idea of a possible extinction was looming.

The game was important to both sides who didn't want to lose. A goalless first half meant that there were only 45 minutes for either team to risk attacking and get the win. Chelsea needed the win more and a magical moment appeared with twenty minutes to go. Blues winger Clive Walker received the ball outside the area and struck a shot that flew past Bolton keeper Seamus McDonagh. It gave his team the lead and ended up being the only goal of the game, giving Chelsea all three points and pushed them up to 14th.

Chelsea managed to survive relegation that season after finishing 18th. Bolton ended up finishing bottom of the table and would be joined by Burnley and Rotherham in next season's Third Division. Clive Walker's goal is arguably the most important ever scored in the club's history.

GAME 53
The first penalty shootout

Chelsea 0 Leicester 2
(Won 4-3 on penalties)
25th October 1983

League Cup Round 2 (2nd Leg)
Stamford Bridge
Chelsea; Eddie Niedzwiecki, John Hollins, Joey Jones, Colin Pates, Joe McLaughlin, David Speedie, Paul Canoville, Nigel Spackman, Kerry Dixon, Colin Lee, Pat Nevin
Penalty Shoot-out; Dixon (scored), Hollins (scored), Speedie (saved), Spackman (scored), Lee (scored)
Manager; John Neal
Referee; Lester C Shapter
Attendance; 15,646

Chelsea started their 1983/84 season in Division Two but were in scintillating form. On the opening day of the season they thrashed Derby 5-0 at Stamford Bridge. There were debuts for Chelsea stars of the future Kerry Dixon, Nigel Spackman, Eddie Niedzwiecki and Joe McLaughlin. Dixon (2) and Spackman managed to get on the score sheet.

The Blues won won four of their next five games including a 5-1 aggregate win in the League Cup against Gillingham. Their reward for winning was a tie against Division One side Leicester City. The Foxes hadn't started their season brightly as they had lost seven out of eight league games. Things didn't get any better when Chelsea went up to Filbert Street at the beginning of October. John Neal's side won 2-0 with first half goals from Dixon and Paul Canoville.

Chelsea welcomed Leicester to Stamford Bridge for the second leg. Leicester were still winless in their league campaign so things were looking good for the home side to progress into the next round. However, football is rarely as straight forward as that. Alan Smith put the visitors ahead in the first half to cut the deficit to 2-1.

Leicester had made a substitution in the game seeing Tommy English replace Ian Banks which proved to be a smart move as he scored a second goal for the visitors in the final ten minutes. Referee Lester Shapter blew the final whistle which left the scores level at 2-2 on aggregate. Due to a change of football rules, a penalty shootout would be needed to determine a winner. This was the first penalty shoot out in the Blues history.

Kerry Dixon stepped up first and slotted the ball home to give Chelsea a 1-0 lead. Leicester's Steve Lynex was next but his penalty was saved by goalkeeper Eddie Niedzwiecki. John Hollins and Tommy English both scored for their clubs before David Speedie saw his spot kick saved by Mark Wallington. Bob Hazell made the scores level and then Nigel Spackman and Peter Eastoe both netted to make it 3-3 after four penalties each.

Chelsea's fifth penalty was to be taken by Colin Lee who had only taken one penalty for the Blues, vs Shrewsbury Town in January 1981. He scored that time and it was the same outcome in the shootout. Kevin MacDonald was Leicester's final penalty taker but Niedzwiecki was the hero as his save meant his side had won the penalty shootout 4-3. Unfortunately a 1-0 loss to West Brom in the next round ended their League Cup run.

GAME 54
Going up

Grimsby Town 0 Chelsea 1
12th May 1984

Football League Division Two
Blundell Park
Chelsea; Eddie Niedzwiecki, John Hollins, Dale Jasper, Colin Pates, Joe McLaughlin, John Bumstead, Pat Nevin, Nigel Spackman, Kerry Dixon, David Speedie, Micky Thomas
Scorer; Dixon
Manager; John Neal
Referee; John Hunting
Attendance; 13,000

Chelsea had been stuck in Division Two for five seasons. Their flirtation with relegation the previous campaign didn't give many Blues fans much to look forward to. John Neal had managed to sign some new players in the summer but the arrival of Mickey Thomas from Stoke later in season was an important signing in the completion of his team.

At the end of 1983 Chelsea found themselves sitting in first place after a 1-0 win against Brighton on New Years Eve. Two weeks later Thomas made his debut in a 2-1 win at Derby and the following game he netted his first (and second) goal in his Blues career. Chelsea continued the rest of the season see-sawing between first and second in the league battling it out with Sheffield Wednesday for top spot.

On the final day of the season Chelsea were joint top of the league with the Owls, separated only by the Blues' superior goal difference. A win would see them crowned Second Division champions and a place back in the top flight again. Sheffield Wednesday were to play Cardiff City and comfortably won 2-0 to give them all three points.

Chelsea travelled to Grimsby to play in front of a crowd of 13,000 at Blundell Park. The Blues started brightly and it was top marksman Kerry Dixon who headed his team into a 1-0 lead just before half time. This ended up being the final score despite Chelsea being awarded a penalty that was saved from Pat Nevin. It didn't matter though and John Neal's men had won promotion back into the First Division after being crowned champions on goal difference.

GAME 55
Chelsea are back

Arsenal 1 Chelsea 1
25th August 1984

Football League Division One
Highbury
Chelsea; Eddie Niedzwiecki, Colin Lee, Doug Rougvie, Colin Pates, Joe McLaughlin, Dale Jasper, Pat Nevin, Nigel Spackman, Kerry Dixon, David Speedie, Paul Canoville
Scorer; Dixon
Manager; John Neal
Referee; Alan Robinson
Attendance; 45,329

It was 1984 and Chelsea were in the top flight for the first time in six years. The club were where they belonged and the fans were excited about the season ahead. In that summer the Blues signed Doug Rougvie from Aberdeen for £150,000.

The league fixtures for the 1984/85 season were announced and Chelsea's opening game was a trip to London rivals Arsenal at Highbury with an 11:30am kick off following orders from the police. A crowd of 45,000 people watched the match and it was reported that 20k of those were Chelsea fans. There were many touts around the ground which is why so many Blues fans made it into the game.

Chelsea were without Welshmen Mickey Thomas and Joey Jones through suspension and John Bumstead was injured. The atmosphere at the game was electric. Dale Jasper almost gave the visitors the lead when his turn and shot from outside the box was pushed aside by Pat Jennings. Eddie

117

Niedzwiecki made save after save for his side to keep the score level at 0-0.

Arsenal took the lead after 35 minutes when Pat Nevin had given away a freekick. Captain Kenny Samson provided the delivery and Paul Mariner scored a header in front of the North Bank. However, the Gooners were not celebrating for long. Four minutes later Chelsea were awarded a freekick of their own. Doug Rougvie's long ball forward was met by Kerry Dixon whose left footed shot was saved by Jennings but it was only parried back out to the Chelsea striker who smashed in a right footed volley. The Clock End erupted as the Blues fans were going wild. Chelsea had equalised. This was one of the most iconic goals in the club's history and has been well documented in other books.

The second half saw a few half chances for both sides but none of these were converted into goals and the game ended 1-1. The highlight in the second half was when Arsenal were on the attack. Their new signing and England international Viv Anderson received a ball in the Chelsea half but a slightly heavy touch allowed Rougvie to put in a huge challenge, winning the ball cleanly but leaving Anderson on the deck. This was the start of the cult hero status of Doug Rougvie amongst Blues fans. Chelsea were buoyant and with reason. They ended the season finishing sixth in the division, their highest position since 1971.

GAME 56
The magic of the League Cup

Sheffield Wednesday 4 Chelsea 4
(After Extra Time. Score at 90 mins 4-4)
30th January 1985

League Cup Round Quarter-Final (Replay)
Hillsborough
Chelsea; Eddie Niedzwiecki, Joey Jones, Doug Rougvie, Colin Lee (Paul Canoville 46), Joe McLaughlin, Dale Jasper, Pat Nevin, Nigel Spackman, Kerry Dixon, David Speedie, Micky Thomas
Scorers; Canoville (2), Dixon, Thomas
Booked; Jones, Nevin, Rougvie, Lee
Manager; John Neal
Referee; George Tyson
Attendance; 36,505

Chelsea were looking good in the league and wanted to put a decent cup run together as they hadn't reached a semi final since 1973. The Blues were drawn against Millwall in the League Cup, known at the time as the Milk Cup. Chelsea won the first leg 3-1 with a brace from Kerry Dixon after former blue Michael Nutton scored an own goal. A 1-1 draw in the second leg ensured that Chelsea would go through 4-2 on aggregate and meet Walsall in the next round.

Walsall welcomed Chelsea to Fellows Park and a crowd of just over 11,000 saw a back and forth game which ended 2-2 after the Blues equalised twice through Pat Nevin and Colin Lee. A replay was needed but John Neal's men cruised to 3-0 victory after David Speedie, Dixon and Joey Jones all scored within the first fifteen minutes of the match. Man City awaited a trip to Stamford Bridge after that but the visitors were thrashed 4-1 courtesy of a hattrick from Dixon before Jones scored a fourth. Pat Nevin even had a penalty saved after Paul Canoville was fouled by keeper Alex Williams with the scoreline 4-0. This was one of the worst penalties taken in the Blues history. The Scotsman took one step and his tamely struck spot kick was gathered by the City keeper.

In the Milk Cup fifth round Chelsea were awarded a home fixture against Sheffield Wednesday. The Owls took a first half lead through Lawrie Madden's header. However, David Speedie headed an equaliser for the home side ten minutes later following a corner kick. The score ended 1-1 which meant a replay at Hillsborough was needed.

A crowd of 36,000 came to watch what would be one of the most thrilling games of football ever seen. The home side were on fire as they stormed into a 3-0 lead by half time. Chelsea's Paul Canoville was sitting in the dugout with Keith Jones. A Sheffield Wednesday supporter had been goading them both and even offered them a sweet when Wednesday took the lead. John Neal brought Canoville on at half time who provided an instant impact as the tricky winger scored 11 seconds into the half. Instead of celebrating with fans or players he just ran back to the dugout area to find the woman who had offered him a sweet.

Chelsea got another goal back with 25 minutes to play after Dixon netted his 28th of the season. The comeback was on, and in fact, ten minutes later Nigel Spackman in the heart of the Blues midfield tussled in his own half before breaking free. He passed it to Speedie who quickly gave it to Nevin. It was the Scottish winger's run and turn on the edge of the box that allowed Mickey Thomas to find space and smash the ball home from the 18 yard line. The score was now 3-3 with quarter of an hour to go.

Both sides were looking tired but the fresh legs of Canoville were to provide fruitful for his side because with five minutes to go Dixon received the ball and played in the substitute whose delicate chip over Martin Hodge put them 4-3 up from a 3-0 deficit at half time. Surely that was enough for John Neal's men. Unfortunately, Wednesday were awarded a penalty in the final minute when Doug Rougvie fouled Mel Sterland and the man who was tripped struck his penalty right down the middle as Niedzwiecki dived to his right. A further 30 minutes extra time was played but no goals were scored.

A second replay at Stamford Bridge was played and it was Sheffield Wednesday who took a 12 minute lead. Chelsea were later awarded a freekick on the half hour mark and Pat Nevin's quick thinking and skill allowed him to trick the visitor's defence and put in a delightful cross for Speedie to head in at the back post. In the final minute of the game Mickey Thomas headed his side into the semi finals from a corner taken by Paul Canoville.

In the summer before this season Chelsea said goodbye to Clive Walker as he moved to Sunderland for £75,000. This proved to be a costly move as Walker scored twice against his former side in the League Cup semi final, denying the Blues a trip to Wembley.

GAME 57
The first Wembley win

Chelsea 5 Man City 4
23rd March 1986

Full Members Cup Final
Wembley
Chelsea; Steve Francis, Darren Wood, Doug Rougvie, Colin Pates, Joe McLaughlin, John Bumstead, Pat Nevin, Nigel Spackman, Colin Lee, David Speedie, Kevin McAllister
Scorers; Speedie (3), Lee (2)
Manager; John Hollins
Referee; Alan Saunders
Attendance; 67,236

In 1985 a new cup competition was introduced called the Full Members' Cup. It was created after English clubs were banned from European football following the Heysel Stadium disaster where 39 people died. The competition was for all clubs in England's top two divisions but excluded the six sides who qualified for Europe as they played in the English Super Cup. The idea for the Full Members' Cup came from Chelsea chairman Ken Bates.

In its inaugural season the Blues were drawn against Portsmouth who were beaten 3-0 at Stamford Bridge in front of a crowd of just 6,833. John Bumstead and Micky Hazard gave the home side a 2-0 lead after five minutes before Kerry Dixon scored towards the end of the game. They then beat Charlton 3-1 at Selhurst Park before facing West Brom at The Hawthorns. A pitiful crowd of around 4,000 saw the sides draw 2-2. A penalty shootout was needed which Chelsea won 5-4. Substitute Colin Lee hit the decisive penalty to send his team into the semi final and a two-legged affair with Oxford United.

Things didn't start well for the Blues as Keith Jones was sent off just before the half hour mark. However, shortly after Neil Slatter put the ball in his own net to give Chelsea a 1-0 advantage leading into half time. Dixon made it 2-0 but Oxford did mount a fight back as John Aldridge converted a penalty with ten minutes to go. It was short lived though as Dixon added a second and then completed his hattrick to take a 4-1 lead back to Stamford Bridge. Although Oxford did win 1-0 in the return leg it wasn't enough and Chelsea were rewarded with a trip to Wembley to face Man City in the final.

Even though the previous rounds were not taken seriously by fans there was definite interest in a Wembley showdown as 67,000 people were in attendance that day. A strange occurrence was that both teams played in their away kits for the match, Chelsea wearing an all white kit with thin blue and red hoops.

Man City took the lead after ten minutes through Steve Kinsey following a freekick. They held their lead until Pat Nevin received the ball on the left hand side and crossed the ball on to David Speedie's head which went past Eric Nixon in the City goal from six yards. Colin Lee then made it 2-1 to the 'Whites' after some scrappy play but it was enough to give John Hollins' men the advantage at half time.

The second half was full of excitement as Chelsea went on to take a 5-1 lead with Speedie getting a hattrick (the first at Wembley since Geoff Hurst in 1966) and Colin Lee doubling his tally with ten minutes to go. Chelsea fans in attendance were in fine voice and confident.

There was late drama as Man City scored what looked to be a consolation goal when Mark Lillis headed home with five minutes to play. However, with two minutes left Doug Rougvie scored an own goal to make it 5-3. The Chelsea defence and fans were starting to get a little nervy and this was further compounded when Mark Lillis was brought down in the Chelsea box. The midfielder took the resulting penalty and slotted it coolly into the corner to make it 5-4. Luckily for the Blues referee Alan Saunders blew his whistle shortly after and Chelsea were crowned the first ever Full Members' Cup winners. Colin Pates became part of an elite group of Chelsea captains that have lifted silverware, and the first to do it at Wembley.

GAME 58
The Premier League begins

Chelsea 1 Oldham 1
15th August 1992

Premier League
Stamford Bridge
Chelsea; Dave Beasant, Steve Clarke, Gareth Hall, Vinnie Jones, Paul Elliott, Mal Donaghy, Graham Stuart, Robert Fleck, Mick Harford, Andy Townsend, Damien Matthew (Eddie Newton 76)
Scorer; Harford
Booked; Harford
Manager; Ian Porterfield
Referee; Jim Borrett
Attendance; 20,699

By the late 1980s football attendances were falling, hooliganism was rife, stadiums were becoming less fit for purpose and English teams were banned from playing in European competition. It was not a good time for the home of football. They were behind other leagues such as La Liga and Serie A with some of the top stars deciding to move abroad to further their careers. However, a few clubs noticed the business potential of football clubs and threatened to break away from the football league to compete in a Super League.

In the early 1990s a deal had been struck which involved the start of the Premier League. The format and the teams didn't change from previous years, just the way revenue could be generated and shared between the clubs in the top flight through TV money. Chelsea finished the 1991/92 season in 14th spot guaranteeing them a place in the inaugural Premier League consisting of 22 clubs.

On the 15th of August Chelsea welcomed Oldham Athletic to Stamford Bridge to play in their first ever Premier League game. The Blues gave debuts to Northern Ireland's Mal Donaghy at the age of 34, the club's £2.1m record signing Robert Fleck from Norwich and striker Mick Harford from Luton. They were not the only changes as referee's now wore green, teams were allowed to name three substitutes and the backpass rule was introduced.

Robert Fleck impressed early on as his attempt on goal forced a good save from the Latics keeper John Hallworth after 20 minutes. He also narrowly missed later in the first half as his lobbed effort went wide of the post. It wasn't enough though and both sides went into the half time break scoreless.

In the second half Chelsea took the lead through debutant Harford when his shot from 25 yards flew past the Oldham keeper with only five minutes left to play. It looked like the home side would take all three points until two minutes later. Nick Henry received the ball and struck it from 40 yards out towards the Shed End. Chelsea keeper Dave Beasant made a calamitous mistake giving the ball away cheaply and was unable to get back in time to stop it.

GAME 59
Run, Spencer, run

Austria Wien 1 Chelsea 1
20th October 1994

UEFA Cup Winners Cup Round 2 (2nd Leg)
Franz Horr Stadium
Chelsea; Dmitri Kharine, Erland Johnsen, John Spencer, Dennis Wise, Andy Myers, Nigel Spackman, Eddie Newton, Neil Shipperley, David Rocastle (Glenn Hoddle 80), Anthony Barness, Gareth Hall (Scott Minto 46)
Scorer; Spencer
Player Manager; Glenn Hoddle
Referee; F Vandenwijngaert
Attendance; 25,000

In the 1993/94 season Chelsea were under the leadership of Glenn Hoddle who guided the club to their first FA Cup final since 1970. They played Man Utd who they'd already beaten twice in the league that season. Gavin Peacock scored in both games as the Blues ran out 1-0 winners. However, the FA Cup final was a different story as Chelsea lost 4-0 where the refereeing was as poor as the weather on a rain soaked Saturday afternoon. Man Utd won the league that season and would enter the Champions League as a reward. The Blues did qualify for the European Cup Winners Cup though as runners up.

Chelsea faced Viktoria Zizkov from the Czech Republic in the first round. The opening leg was played at Stamford Bridge and fans had waited nearly 25 years since their last European outing. A crowd of just over 22,000 saw the home side cruise to a 4-2 victory after summer signings Paul Furlong and David Rocastle added to goals from Frank Sinclair and Dennis Wise. The away leg was a much less eventful game although Dmitri Kharine did save a penalty from Petr Vrabec 30 minutes into the match.

In the next round Chelsea faced Austria Wien, again with the first leg at Stamford Bridge. Glenn Hoddle was without Steve Clarke, Scott Minto and John Spencer through injury. Dennis Wise had also recently been stripped of the captaincy due to an off the field incident involving a taxi. To make matters even worse Frank Sinclair sustained an injury after 12 minutes and was replaced by Anthony Barness (who was later replaced by Graham Rix, the man that turned 37 a few days later). The game ended 0-0 but the visitors had Manfred Schmid sent off for a second yellow card after fouling Dennis Wise.

Chelsea knew that they would face a tough test in the return leg but were boosted by the fact that John Spencer was back and in the starting line up. Austria Wien attacked the Blues and won a corner in the 39th minute. The ball was crossed in but blocked by Erland Johnsen. The ball then fell nicely to Spencer halfway in his own half. He took a positive touch forwards and headed towards the Wien goal. To his surprise there were no defenders ahead of him as they had all come forward for the corner. The wee Scotsman took a little look over his shoulder and knew he was in a straight race towards Franz Wohlfahrt's goal. Spencer carried the ball 80 yards before meeting the Austrian who had hesitated and stayed on his six yard line. The Chelsea forward rounded the shot stopper and coolly slotted the ball home to give his side a 1-0 lead. It was one of the greatest goals scored in the Blues history. After his 80 yard run he celebrated by running another 80 yards in the opposite direction.

Austria Wien did mount a fightback and managed to get an equaliser with 15 minutes to go through Arminas Narbekovas. However, it was not enough and Glenn Hoddle's men progressed to the next round on the away goals rule. Chelsea did march on through the competition until they were unable to overturn a 3-0 semi final first leg defeat to Real Zaragoza from Spain. The score in the second leg was 3-1 to the Blues, losing 4-3 on aggregate. The

Spanish side did go on to win the competition beating London rivals Arsenal 2-1 in the final. Former Spurs midfielder Nayim scored from the halfway line in the last minute of extra time to seal the victory for his team.

GAME 60
Glenn's goodbye

Chelsea 2 Blackburn 3
5th May 1996

Premier League
Stamford Bridge
Chelsea; Dmitri Kharine, Scott Minto, Ruud Gullit, Erland Johnsen, John Spencer, Mark Hughes, Dennis Wise, Craig Burley (Dan Petrescu 64), Andy Myers, Nigel Spackman (Gavin Peacock 67), David Lee (Paul Furlong 90)
Scorers; Wise, Spencer
Booked; Johnsen, Wise
Manager; Glenn Hoddle
Referee; Martin J Bodenham
Attendance; 28,436

Chelsea under Glenn Hoddle were starting to go places and make people stand up and notice the sleeping giant. Although their league form was still inconsistent the talent they were attracting was of a genuine class not seen at the Bridge in a long time. The Blues secured the talent of Man Utd and Wales legend Mark Hughes for £1.5m. However, the biggest shock signing of the summer came when Chelsea announced that former World Player of the Year, Ruud Gullit, had signed on a free transfer from Sampdoria. To date this is still one of the greatest transfers in Premier League history.

The Blues started the season with a home game against Everton. Stamford Bridge was awash with Gullit wigs being sold outside the ground. There was a real feeling that it might have been a season to remember. However, the game was less memorable as it ended 0-0.

Chelsea finished 11th in the league for a second season running but did get to the FA Cup semi final. They lost 2-1 to Man Utd with Ruud Gullit giving his side a 1-0 lead at Villa Park before Andy Cole equalised and David Beckham capitalised on a disasterous back pass from Craig Burley. Despite that, Glenn Hoddle was rising stock in the managerial world and his talent was noticed by the English FA. Soon after the Football Association announced that Glenn Hoddle would take over from former blue Terry Venables as the new England manager at the end of the campaign.

On the final day of the season Chelsea welcomed Blackburn Rovers to Stamford Bridge and the visitors enjoyed their time as they ran out 3-2 winners. However, the Blues fans knew that their manager was leaving and spent most of the match showing their appreciation for what Hoddle had started as well as their thoughts on who the next manager should be. There were rumours that former blue, and Arsenal manager, George Graham was set to take over but the fans inside Stamford Bridge let the board know where they should stick that idea. The supporters alternative choice was that of superstar Ruud Gullit. Their wish came true as the Dutchman was announced as the Blues boss. Hoddle was the end of the first stage of Chelsea's rise to notoriety and Gullit was the next stage looking to include silverware.

GAME 61
In memory of Matthew Harding

Chelsea 3 Tottenham 1
26th October 1996

Premier League
Stamford Bridge
Chelsea; Kevin Hitchcock, Dan Petrescu, Ruud Gullit (Craig Burley 73), Steve Clarke (Erland Johnsen 59), Gianluca Vialli, Mark Hughes, Dennis Wise, Michael Duberry, David Lee (Terry Phelan 79), Roberto Di Matteo, Scott Minto
Scorers; Gullit, Lee, Di Matteo
Booked; Petrescu, Wise
Manager; Ruud Gullit
Referee; Roger Dilkes
Attendance; 28,373

The 1996/97 season was one of the most exciting in Chelsea history. Ruud Gullit had been appointed the new manager and the Blues had signed Frank Leboeuf, Roberto Di Matteo and Gianluca Vialli in the summer. One of the reasons that the club were able to make these signings was the financial backing from Matthew Harding. He was a lifelong Chelsea fan and successful businessman who responded to a call from chairman Ken Bates for investment a few years earlier.

Matthew Harding invested over £25m into the club and became a member of the board. Over the coming years Bates and Harding frequently clashed over the direction of the club and Harding was banned from the boardroom. He did have the support of former manager Glenn Hoddle and was a favourite amongst Chelsea fans.

On the 22nd October the Blues travelled to Bolton for a League Cup game on a Tuesday night. The Lancashire side were in the division below but pulled off a shock 2-1 win. Scott Minto put the visitors in front after just two minutes but goals from John McGinlay and Nathan Blake booked their place in the next round. This was not expected but a bigger shock happened that night. After the game Matthew Harding and three friends flew back from the game in a helicopter. However, poor weather made things difficult to travel. Tragedy struck when the pilot lost control and the helicopter crashed, killing Harding and his friends.

The news of Harding's death was hard to take and many Chelsea fans were upset. A memorial to Matthew was set up at Stamford Bridge for people to lay flowers, shirts and scarves to pay their respects to the lifelong Blues fan. Chelsea's next fixture was against London rivals Tottenham. There were discussions about postponing the game but it was decided it should have gone ahead as it's what he would have wanted.

Chelsea welcomed Spurs to Stamford Bridge. The players came out wearing black armbands to show their respects. The Tottenham players stood around the centre circle whilst the Blues stood on the edge of the penalty area facing the newly built North Stand, funded by Matthew Harding. The players held hands during an impeccably observed minute silence. After this fans began chanting 'There's only one Matthew Harding' in fine voice just before kick off.

Player/Manager Ruud Gullit started his first game of the season at Stamford Bridge and was an inspired decision as the he put the Blues ahead just before the half hour mark. Tottenham's Chris Armstrong equalised before halftime with a header. In the second half Dan Petrescu won a penalty for Chelsea which David Lee confidently put away past Ian Walker. Roberto Di Matteo made it 3-1 with ten minutes to go and the Blues won all three points. However, this game will be fondly remembered for the legacy of Matthew Harding. The newly built North Stand was quickly named the

Matthew Harding Stand and is where the noisier and more vocal fans tend to congregate. To this day they still sing his name at every game. 'Matthew Harding's Blue and White Army!

GAME 62
The FA Cup comeback

Chelsea 4 Liverpool 2
26th January 1997

FA Cup Round 4

Stamford Bridge

Chelsea; Kevin Hitchcock, Dan Petrescu, Frank Leboeuf, Steve Clarke, Gianluca Vialli, Dennis Wise, Roberto Di Matteo, Scott Minto (Mark Hughes 46), Frank Sinclair, Eddie Newton, Gianfranco Zola

Scorers; Vialli (2), Hughes, Zola

Booked; Sinclair, Wise

Manager; Ruud Gullit

Referee; Steve W Dunn

Attendance; 27,950

Chelsea beat West Brom 3-0 in the third round of the FA Cup with goals from Dennis Wise, Craig Burley and new signing Gianfranco Zola. In the game before this the Blues played Liverpool in the league and won 1-0 thanks to Roberto Di Matteo's strike when Liverpool midfielder Michael Thomas sloppily gave the ball away which the Italian put away from just outside the box. The two sides would then meet in the FA Cup fourth round, again at Stamford Bridge.

The Blues welcomed Liverpool who were sitting top of the Premier League at the time. Robbie Fowler and British transfer record Stan Collymore were leading the Merseysiders attack. It was these two players that gave Liverpool a 2-0 lead at half time although it could have been more if not for Liverpool's poor finishing and superb goalkeeping from Kevin Hitchcock.

At half time the Chelsea players walked into the dressing room awaiting a

139

few choice words from manager Ruud Gullit. However, the dreadlocked superstar just sat there and read a newspaper. The players looked a little perplexed until the boss put the paper down. He then went on to explain that they would go on to win the game. All they needed to do was to stop John Barnes getting the ball in the Liverpool midfield. Also, he decided to make a substitution by taking off defender Scott Minto for FA Cup veteran Mark Hughes who had won the competition three times.

Mark Hughes' introduction at half time was an inspired change as the Welshman scored within five minutes after he used his strength to hold off Liverpool's defence before turning and hitting the ball past David James. Less than ten minutes later it was the little Italian magician Zola that hit a curling shot from outside the box after Hughes' lay off. These two players had built a fantastic relationship on the pitch which had left Ginaluca Vialli out of the regular starting line up. Chelsea were now level with the visitors and on the ascendency.

Gianluca Vialli was starting his first Chelsea game since the beginning of December and he intended to show his manager that he had a lot to offer the team. Just after the hour mark Dan Petrescu received the ball and played it forward to Vialli who poked the ball home from 15 yards to put his side 3-2 up. With fifteen minutes to go the Blues were awarded a freekick. Zola's ball into the box was met by the head of Vialli and it flew into the net in front of advertising boarding. The Shed End was being rebuilt but the rest of the ground made up for it in terms of noise. From 2-0 down at half time the Blues won 4-2 against the league leaders and ensured their name would be in the hat for the next round draw.

GAME 63
Sent to Coventry (without the right kit)

Coventry 3 Chelsea 1
9th April 1997

Premier League
Highfield Road

Chelsea; Frode Grodas, Frank Leboeuf, Steve Clarke, Mark Hughes (Danny Granville 85), Craig Burley, Roberto Di Matteo, Scott Minto, Frank Sinclair, Eddie Newton, Gianfranco Zola, Paul Hughes (Gianluca Vialli 62)

Scorer; P Hughes

Booked; Di Matteo, Minto, Sinclair

Manager; Ruud Gullit

Referee; Dermot J Gallagher

Attendance; 19,917

In April 1997 Chelsea played Coventry City at Highfield Road. The Blues had lost their previous two games without scoring. The game away against Coventry came four days before their FA Cup semi final match up vs Wimbledon.

Coventry were sitting one place above the relegation zone and only three points off the bottom. They had beaten Liverpool at Anfield at the weekend and were looking to build on this result against Chelsea. Manager Ruud Gullit made five changes to the starting line up including youth team product Paul Hughes playing midfield. However, there were tensions in the dressing room, especially between Gullit and Gianluca Vialli. The Dutchman had criticised the Italian's performance from the previous game which Vialli took exception to on Italian TV. The Chelsea striker was dropped to the bench despite the lack of fitness to Gianfranco Zola.

The game started well for the Blues as Paul Hughes put them ahead just before half time. However, their lead didn't last long as Dion Dublin equalised early in the second half and Paul Williams put them ahead two minutes later. Noel Whelan made it 3-1 to the Sky Blues around the hour mark. Coventry's performance was inspired by player/manager Gordon Strachan who had made his first start for almost a year at the age of 40.

It wasn't the result or style of play that made this game memorable. The real reason were decisions made by referee Dermot Gallagher and the Chelsea kitman. The Blues travelled up to Coventry but Gallagher felt that Chelsea and Coventry's shades of blue clashed and forced the visitors to wear a different kit. However, as Chelsea hadn't brought their away kit they had two options, either to forfeit the match or wear Coventry's black and red checkered strip. Ruud Gullit's team accepted the compromise. It was reported that Blues defender Frank Leboeuf took off the shirt at the end of the game, threw it to the floor and spat on it.

GAME 64
The 1997 FA Cup final

Chelsea 2 Middlesbrough 0
17th May 1997

FA Cup Final
Wembley
Chelsea; Frode Grodas, Dan Petrescu, Frank Leboeuf, Steve Clarke, Mark Hughes, Dennis Wise, Roberto Di Matteo, Scott Minto, Frank Sinclair, Eddie Newton, Gianfranco Zola (Gianluca Vialli 89)
Scorers; Di Matteo, Newton
Booked; Di Matteo, Leboeuf, Newton
Manager; Ruud Gullit
Referee; Steve J Lodge
Attendance; 79,160

Ruud Gullit has led his team to an FA Cup final after beating Wimbledon at Highbury in the semi final. There was so much excitement and optimism going into the season showpiece at Wembley. The foreign influence on the Chelsea side was instrumental in the cup run. The Blues would play Middlesbrough in the final. Boro had invested heavily in overseas players as well. Fabrizio Ravanelli, who played alongside Chelsea's Gianluca Vialli in the Champions League final for Juventus in the previous season, signed for £7m and scored a hattrick on his league debut. Brazilian midfielder Emerson also signed in the summer to join Juninho.

Chelsea had beaten them 1-0 at Stamford Bridge in the second game of the season with Roberto Di Matteo scoring the goal. The score was reversed at the Riverside Stadium where Juninho netted the only goal of the game. Just before Christmas 1996 Boro did not have enough fit players for a game vs Blackburn and so had to forfeit the match and were deducted three points.

They also sat at the bottom of the table for most of the season. However, their form in cup competitions was much better, reaching the final of the League Cup (losing to Leicester in a replay) and an FA Cup final against the Blues.

Chelsea hadn't won a major trophy in 26 years but the opportunity against Middlesbrough seemed to be too good to miss. The spirit of the cup was in full flow and the team even released an FA Cup final song. The song Blue Day was performed by lifelong Chelsea fan and Madness lead singer, Suggs, and reached number 22 in the charts. Comedian and Middlesbrough fan Bob Mortimer had recorded Boro's cup final song but it didn't chart anywhere near the Blues single.

Gullit walked his team out on to the Wembley pitch looking to banish memories of the 1994 FA Cup final for good. The fans had waited so long to win silverware but they didn't have to wait long to see their team score first. Middlesbrough kicked off and won a throw in inside the Chelsea half. The Teesiders didn't take control of the ball and Dennis Wise nicked it neatly and played the ball to Di Matteo, receiving it in his own half. The Italian midfielder then proceeded to dribble towards the Boro goal. He was given a clear run (maybe helped by a slight body check from Mark Hughes) and struck the ball from 25 yards out. His shot hit the underside of the crossbar and past Ben Roberts in the Middlesbrough goal. Chelsea were ahead after just 43 seconds. It was the quickest ever goal in a Wembley FA Cup Final. Those that were already in their seats were going wild whilst those finishing their beers had no idea what had just happened.

The game continued to be dominated by Chelsea, especially after Ravanelli limped off midway through the first half. Gianluca Festa did manage to get an equaliser but it was later ruled out for offside. With less than ten minutes to go Eddie Newton brought the ball forward before playing it out wide to Dan Petrescu. His cross was then flicked back into the danger area by Gianfranco Zola and Newton finished off the move and Middlesbrough's chances of winning the FA Cup. With just two minutes to play Gullit made a substitution bringing on fan favourite Gianluca Vialli for a taste of the magic of the FA Cup.

Referee Stephen Lodge blew his whistle and the game was done. Chelsea had exorcised their demons and finally won some major silverware. Not only that but Ruud Gullit became the first overseas and black manager to win the FA Cup. Mark Hughes also won his fourth FA Cup winners medal. It wasn't long after that Dennis Wise went up to lift the FA Cup to a huge roar from the Blues fans who had waited so long for this day to come.

After the game Dennis Wise found Roberto Di Matteo and his blind sister. The cheeky captain asked Di Matteo's sister if she'd like him to tell her about her brother's goal. She agreed and he began to tell a story that he ran around the whole of the Middlesbrough team but stopped the ball on the goal line before he invited her brother to come and tap it in. Robbie wasn't too pleased with the antics but his sister saw the funny side of it.

An open top bus parade was organised to drive down the Fulham Road towards the town hall. The streets were filled with Chelsea fans eager to share their happiness with the set of heroes for a new generation. This was the start of many trophies heading to Stamford Bridge over the coming years. Glenn Hoddle had started the project but it was Ruud Gullit who pushed it on to the next level. It was just a shame that the late Matthew Harding was not alive to witness it all.

GAME 65
Snow joke

Tromso 3 Chelsea 2
23rd October 1997

UEFA Cup Winners Cup Round 2 (1st Leg)
Alfheim
Chelsea; Ed De Goey, Celestine Babayaro, Frank Leboeuf (Andy Myers 87), Steve Clarke, Gianluca Vialli, Dennis Wise, Roberto Di Matteo, Danny Granville (Mark Hughes 46), Frank Sinclair, Eddie Newton, Gianfranco Zola
Scorer; Vialli (2)
Manager; Ruud Gullit
Referee; Jacek Granat
Attendance; 6,438

Nowadays technology and TV money have meant that football is scheduled to play throughout the year, whatever the weather. Gone are the days when teams had to postpone games for about a month during the winter due to the state of their pitches. Rarely is a game cancelled due to pitch conditions, especially in the top leagues.

After winning the 1997 FA Cup Chelsea were awarded a spot in the UEFA Cup Winners Cup. The Blues knew they had to bolster their squad if they were to continue with the good work they had put in. Managing Director, Colin Hutchison, worked tirelessly over the summer to secure the signings of Gus Poyet, Tore Andre Flo and the re-signing of England leftback and Chelsea youth product Graeme Le Saux for £5,000,000. Other signings included Ed De Goey, Celestine Babayaro, Bernard Lambourde and Laurent Charvet (on loan from Cannes).

In the first round of the cup they faced Slovan Bratislava from Slovakia. They won both legs 2-0 with Danny Granville and Roberto Di Matteo scoring at Stamford Bridge and Di Matteo and Gianluca Villi getting the goals in the away leg. Chelsea would play Norwegian side Tromso, the northernmost top-level football club in the world.

The Blues travelled to Tromso to play in front of a crowd less than 7,000. It was the home side who took a shock 2-0 lead into the half time interval. However, this wasn't the biggest shock of the game. During halftime heavy snow fell and completely covered the pitch. Chelsea manager Ruud Gullit argued that the game should be abandoned but referee Jacek Granat disagreed and the game resumed. Play did have to be suspended twice so that ground staff could redraw the lines by using brooms to sweep away the snow.

Gianluca Vialli provided hope for his side as his goal with five minutes to go halved the deficit. The Blues wanted to make a substitution straight after but the referee said no. Unfortunately for Gullit's men Tromso made it 3-1 a minute later but Vialli wasn't done yet. His clever footwork and calm composure allowed him to dink past the Norwegian defence and poke the ball home to make it 3-2. Two weeks later Chelsea easily won the second leg 7-1 earning a quarter final match up against Real Betis from Spain.

GAME 66

A champagne moment

Chelsea 3 Arsenal 1
18th February 1998

League Cup Semi-Final (2nd leg)
Stamford Bridge
Chelsea; Ed De Goey, Dan Petrescu, Frank Leboeuf, Steve Clarke, Gianluca Vialli (Eddie Newton 80), Mark Hughes, Dennis Wise, Michael Duberry, Graeme Le Saux, Roberto Di Matteo, Gianfranco Zola
Scorers; Hughes, Di Matteo, Petrescu
Booked; Clarke, Duberry, Wise, Hughes
Manager; Gianluca Vialli
Referee; Graham Poll
Attendance; 34,330

In the 1997/98 season Chelsea were putting a title charge together and spent most of the time flirting between 2nd and 3rd. Although the Blues had lost in the FA Cup third round to Man Utd they were still chasing two major cups; the UEFA Cup Winners Cup and the League Cup.

In the League Cup (known as the Coca-Cola Cup) Chelsea had overcome Blackburn (by penalties) and Southampton (after extra time) in the early rounds. Both of these games were at Stamford Bridge but the fifth round away to Ipswich was a similar story. The Blues won 4-1 on penalties after a 2-2 draw in normal time. The win meant that they would play Arsenal in a two-legged semi final starting at Highbury.

It was Arsenal who looked the better team in the first leg. The Gooners took a 1-0 lead into the half time interval when Marc Overmars scored past fellow Dutchman Ed De Goey in the Blues goal. Stephen Hughes made it 2-0 just after halftime. Around the hour mark player/manager Ruud Gullit brought on Mark Hughes for Tore Andre Flo and within ten minutes the Welshman had halved the deficit to give Chelsea an important away goal.

A week later the two sides met in a league game at Highbury and it was Stephen Hughes again who did the damage as his brace ensured a 2-0 win for Arsenal and all three points. It was ten days until they met for the cup semi final second leg but a lot changed in that time.

At the end of the 1995/96 season then manager Glenn Hoddle announced he would be leaving his post as Chelsea boss to take on the England job. This left the board with a dilemma about who to appoint for the next campaign. They did not want this to happen again and so after Gullit's fantastic start to his managerial career it was sensible that the club entered into negotiations to tie Gullit down to a long term deal. It was reported that the Dutchman wanted a player/manager contract which included higher wages but the board were refusing to honour this due to the lack of games that Gullit had actually played. After a short while it was obvious that no compromise was going to be made and so the Chelsea hierarchy decided to end their manager's contract.

The club didn't take long to offer the vacant post to another member of the playing squad, Gianluca Vialli, the man Gullit had signed from Juventus. The fans' favourite quickly agreed and his first game involved trying to overcome Arsenal for a place in the final at Wembley against Middlesbrough, the team the Blues beat in the FA Cup final the previous year.

Before the game started new boss Vialli gathered everybody in the changing room and treated his team to a glass of champagne. This was not a typical sort of thing to do but it wasn't a typical sort of situation. Mark Hughes had even more to toast as he had received his MBE from the Queen that morning. To make things even better for the Welsh striker he scored after just ten minutes firing past Alex Manninger at the Shed End.

In the second half Patrick Vieira was sent off after 48 minutes after receiving a second yellow card. Shortly after Chelsea capitalised on the extra man advantage when Hughes then set up Roberto Di Matteo who hit a stunning strike from 30 yards. Two minutes after that the Blues took a 3-0 lead when Dan Petrescu scored from a corner. The game looked over until Michael Duberry gave away a penalty which was converted by Dennis Bergkamp to make it 3-1 with ten minutes to play.

Referee Graham Poll blew his whistle to signal full time and Chelsea had made it to the final. What a start for the new Blues boss, into a cup final after just one match. A month later the Wembley final saw Vialli' side run out 2-0 winners after extra time when Roberto Di Matteo (again) and Frank Sinclair (in his final Chelsea appearance) scored the goals to give the club their second major trophy in a year.

GAME 67
Zola power

Chelsea 1 Stuttgart 0
13th May 1998

UEFA Cup Winners Cup Final
Rasunda Stadium
Chelsea; Ed De Goey, Dan Petrescu, Frank Leboeuf, Steve Clarke, Gus Poyet (Eddie Newton 80), Gianluca Vialli, Dennis Wise, Michael Duberry, Roberto Di Matteo, Danny Granville, Tore Andre Flo (Gianfranco Zola 71)
Scorer; Zola
Sent off; Petrescu
Booked; Wise
Manager; Gianluca Vialli
Referee; Stefano Braschi
Attendance; 30,216

Chelsea were becoming a team known for doing well in cups. They were the current holders of the FA Cup and the League Cup and were looking to add the UEFA Cup Winners Cup to that list. They had reached the semi final with Vicenza from Italy the only team standing between them and the final.

The first leg in Italy came just four days after beating Middlesbrough in the League Cup final in extra time. 1,200 Chelsea fans made the trip to Vicenza and were greeted by two oddities; the first was that there was an all day alcohol ban and the other was a pamphlet that read 'English go home'. However, this was in reference to the Italian's owners rather than the Blues fans.

The Italian cup winners took a 1-0 lead when Lamberto Zauli scored past Ed De Goey in the Blues goal. This turned out to be the only goal of the game with Chelsea unable to get an important away goal. However, Gianluca Vialli was confident that his side could turn it around in the second leg at Stamford Bridge. Roberto Di Matteo was booked in the match which meant he would miss the return through suspension.

On Thursday 16th April there was a special atmosphere around Stamford Bridge. Many people believed that Chelsea would turn the 1-0 deficit around but others remember the previous UEFA Cup Winners Cup semi final a few years earlier. Di Matteo was suspended in the Blues midfield but they were boosted by the recent return of Gustavo Poyet. The Uruguayan started off the season fantastically but suffered a bad injury that kept him out for months. He had come on as a second half substitute in the previous game against Spurs, six months after his injury. He was low on match sharpness but Gianluca Vialli included him in the starting XI.

Just like the first leg Vicenza opened the scoring, Pasquale Luiso netting after 32 minutes and getting an important away goal meaning the Blues needed to score at least three. He celebrated by putting his finger to his lips suggesting that the Chelsea fans needed to be quiet as they were going to be crashing out at the semi final stage. However, 'Motor Mouth' Poyet had other ideas and within three minutes he had drawn his team level.

Both teams remained unchanged after the break. Early in the second half Chelsea were on the attack with Vialli racing down the right-hand side when he put in a cross from the edge of the Vicenza penalty box for Gianfranco Zola, the smallest man in the team, to thump a header past Pierluigi Brivio at the Matthew Harding end. The whole ground erupted and were willing their team to get one more goal.

It was to be a nervy last 40 minutes for both sides. Both managers made substitutions including Mark Hughes replacing Jody Morris with twenty minutes left to play. Five minutes later Ed De Goey gathered the ball from a poor Vicenza attack and looked around the pitch to see who to distribute the ball to. It didn't take the Dutchman long to decide that launching it forward to Hughes was the best option. The Welsh striker battled to win a header 25 yards out and his flick ended up in the Italian's box. Hughes was the quickest to react and hit a left footed strike from just inside the box which flew in and sent the home fans wild. They had done it. From 2-0 down they managed to get 3-2 in front. Vicenza did nearly score in the dying seconds but the heroics of De Goey ensured the Blues would reach another cup final.

Ask anybody that was at this game and they will tell you it was one of the best and most dramatic nights ever seen at Stamford Bridge. The crowd were electric and the atmosphere was something you just became caught up in. The next stop was a final showdown with German side Stuttgart in Stockholm, Sweden at the Rasunda Stadium.

Chelsea finished the 1997/98 league season in fourth place, their highest finishing position since 1970 and a long way from the relegation troubles of the 1980s. However, there was still one game left for the Blues to play; the UEFA Cup Winners Cup final against Stuttgart. The Blues opponents also finished in fourth place in the Bundesliga. 16,000 Chelsea fans travelled to Stockholm to watch the match. After recent wins and performances in cup competitions there was an optimistic mood that was likely mirrored by the players.

Player/manager Gianluca Vialli had some difficult decisions to make in terms of team selection. This was the club's biggest game in nearly thirty years on the European stage. Gianfranco Zola had been suffering with a groin strain and wasn't 100% fit. Vialli had to decide whether he thought the limited fitness of the Italian maestro would be worth the gamble. Also, Mark Hughes had been the hero in the semi final and started every game since then. In the end the Blues boss decided to play Tore Andre Flo instead of Zola and picked himself over Hughes.

Chelsea dominated the early part of the game but the German side played their way back into it. It was Stuttgart who had the first decent chance when Krassimir Balakov hit a fierce shot that was parried away by Ed De Goey. Dennis Wise had the crowd on their feet after his shot was volleyed narrowly wide just before half time but neither side could break the deadlock.

The game remained a tight affair and so Vialli decided that in the 71st minute he would bring on Zola to replace Flo. Stuttgart had a throw in inside their own half and kicked it forward, only to be comfortably met by Danny Granville. His pass found Poyet who laid it off to Wise in the middle of the park. Wise was able to find the feet of Zola but was quickly challenged. However, it ended back at the feet of the Chelsea captain and his vision and quick thinking found Zola who had continued his run towards the goal. It bounced nicely for the little Italian just on the edge of the box and his controlled strike flew past Franz Wohlfahrt and into the back of the net. Zola had only been on the pitch for about 30 seconds but had given his side the lead with the commentator describing the goal as worthy of winning any cup final in the world!

There was still to be more drama as with only five minutes left to play Chelsea's Dan Petrescu was given a straight red card. The Romanian looked confused as well as fans in the stadium. Replays showed that Petrescu went in for a reckless challenge with Murat Yakin but with minimal contact. Referee Stefano Braschi's night was not finished as he also sent off Stuttgart's Gerard Poschner for dissent in stoppage time. The score remained 1-0 and the Blues had lifted their third major trophy in less than 12 months after waiting 26 years to win just one. The kings of Kings Road were quickly becoming the kings of cup competitions. The club had become the only English side to win the UEFA Cup Winners Cup twice.

The team came back to a hero's welcome which will always be fondly remembered by two Chelsea players. Danny Granville had only played 26 time for the Blues, including 19 as a starter, but had picked up a European medal for his short contribution in his last game for Chelsea prior to his transfer to Leeds Utd. Granville was in complete contrast to long serving Scotsman, Steve Clarke. The game was to be his 421st and last ever game as a player. In that time he had seen the club relegated, lose an FA Cup final 4-0 and pick up the Player of the Year for 1994. He would later join Ruud Gullit's backroom staff at Newcastle before coming back to Stamford Bridge and being promoted to Assistant Manager by Jose Mourinho.

GAME 68
A Super Cup triumph

Chelsea 1 Real Madrid 0
28th August 1998

UEFA Super Cup

Stade Louis II

Chelsea; Ed De Goey, Celestine Babayaro, Frank Leboeuf, Marcel Desailly, Pierluigi Casiraghi (Tore Andre Flo 90), Dennis Wise, Michael Duberry, Graeme Le Saux, Roberto Di Matteo (Gus Poyet 64), Albert Ferrer, Gianfranco Zola (Brian Laudrup 83)

Scorer; Poyet

Booked; Babayaro, Ferrer

Manager; Gianluca Vialli

Referee; Marc Batta

Attendance; 9,762

During the summer of 1998 Chelsea were busy in the transfer market. The club said goodbye to Frank Sinclair (Leicester City), Mark Hughes (Southampton), Steve Clarke and Mark Stein. However, they did recruit Marcel Desailly fresh off of his recent World Cup win with France alongside fellow blue Frank Leboeuf. Gianluca Vialli was also looking to improve his attacking options and signed Pierluigi Casiraghi, 17 year old Mikael Forssell and the in demand attacker Brian Laudrup.

Laudrup signed from Glasgow Rangers on a free transfer in the summer. He nearly joined Man Utd but it was Chelsea who had snapped him up quickly. However, it became apparent that the Danish star had reservations and notified the club that he wanted out before even kicking a ball. The board rejected his request and Laudrup stated he was unhappy in London and with the squad rotation policy.

On the 28th August 1998 Brian Laudrup made his Chelsea debut. He came on as a late substitute for Gianfranco Zola. It was against the Champions League winners Real Madrid in the UEFA Super Cup. The Spanish side boasted players like Roberto Carlos, Fernando Hierro and Raul. Their manager was future Blues boss Guus Hiddink.

It was Real Madrid who looked the better side in the first half. Hierro hit the post from a freekick. Predrag Mijatovic also rounded Ed De Goey but his shot from a narrow angle was off target. The first half remained goalless. However, Chelsea came out brighter in the second half with Frank Leboeuf hitting the post and Graeme Le Saux came close.

Just after the hour mark Chelsea manager Gianluca Vialli brought on Gustavo Poyet to replace Roberto Di Matteo in midfield. This proved to be an inspired decision as twenty minutes later it was the Uruguayan who gave his side the lead. Gianfranco Zola had worked hard all game and it was his trickery in the box followed by a lay off to the edge of the box that allowed Poyet to hit the ball calmly past Bodo Illgner in the Real Madrid goal.

The Blues were able to hold on to the 1-0 scoreline and win the UEFA Super Cup. Chelsea had added a new piece of silverware to their ever growing trophy cabinet and the result meant that Gianluca Vialli had become the club's most decorated manager with three major trophies in just six months!

Brian Laudrup still did not settle with his new club. In the UEFA Cup Winners Cup the Blues faced FC Copenhagen where the Dane scored his only Chelsea goal in his final appearance. Ironically his goal knocked the Danish side out of the competition and then signed for the club after the match so he could return to his homeland.

GAME 69
John Terry's debut

Chelsea 4 Aston Villa 1
28th October 1998

League Cup Round 3
Stamford Bridge
Chelsea; Dmitri Kharine, Dan Petrescu (John Terry 86), Celestine Babayaro, Gus Poyet, Gianluca Vialli (Jon Harley 90), Dennis Wise, Michael Duberry, Tore Andre Flo, Bernard Lambourde, Mark Nicholls (Neil Clement 76), Jody Morris
Scorers; Vialli (3), Flo
Sent off; Wise
Booked; Petrescu, Vialli
Manager; Gianluca Vialli
Referee; Graham P Barber
Attendance; 26,790

Chelsea were expected to mount a serious title challenge in the 1998/99 season but were sitting in sixth place by the time they played Aston Villa in the League Cup third round. The Blues had only won one of their last five games. However, they were looking to hold on to their League Cup after beating Middlesbrough in the final in the previous season.

Gianluca Vialli had decided to rest strikers Gianfranco Zola and summer signing Pierluigi Casiraghi. In their place were Tore Andre Flo and the bald headed Italian himself. It didn't start well for the Blues as Mark Draper gave the visitors the lead after just ten minutes. Vialli levelled the score after 32 minutes to make it 1-1 heading into half time. Later on the player/manager bagged a hattrick for himself and his Norwegian strike partner Flo also scored as the Blues won 4-1 on the night.

In the 86th minute Chelsea made a substitution with Dan Petrescu making way. The Romanian was not happy with the decision and showed his frustration to the Blues bench. He was replaced by 17 year old defender John Terry who was making his debut for the club. Little did fans know that this boy would eventually go on to be the captain, leader, legend that supporters have loved. Terry went on the play 717 times for his club, becoming the highest goalscoring defender. He also won the Premier League, Champions League, Europa League, FA Cup, League Cup and many other team and individual awards. Not only did he captain Chelsea over 400 times and but he wore the armband for England 34 times, making him the sixth in the country's all time list.

A minute after Terry's debut captain Dennis Wise was sent off for a two-footed challenge on Aston Villa's Darren Byfield. This was his fourth red card for the Blues and would go on to be sent off a further four times in his Chelsea career.

The Blues were knocked out in the fifth round by Wimbledon, losing 2-1 at Selhurst Park. Gianluca Vialli got the only Chelsea goal which was his sixth in the competition. This goal tally meant he finished as the league cup golden boot winner in his final season as a professional footballer.

GAME 70
Champions League debut

Chelsea 3 Skonto Riga 0
11th August 1999

UEFA Champions League Preliminary Round (1st Leg)
Stamford Bridge

Chelsea; Ed De Goey, Dan Petrescu (Bjarne Goldbaek 77), Frank Leboeuf, Marcel Desailly, Didier Deschamps (Celestine Babayaro 65), Gus Poyet, Chris Sutton, Dennis Wise, Graeme Le Saux, Albert Ferrer, Gianfranco Zola (Tore Andre Flo 65)

Scorers; Babayaro, Poyet, Sutton
Booked; Sutton
Manager; Gianluca Vialli
Referee; Urs Meier
Attendance; 22,043

In 1955 Chelsea won the league for the only time in their history and by the end of the century that stat hadn't been matched. The introduction of the European Cup in 1955 was an international competition for the league winners from around the continent. The Blues were set to compete as the first English representative but the Football Association saw the tournament as a distraction from domestic competition and banned Chelsea from joining.

In 1992 the European Cup evolved including rebranding it as the Champions League. Rather than a straight knockout competition it changed to the current format of a group stage before elimination. Also, in 1997 the tournament included the runners up in some domestic leagues, including England. At the end of the 1998/99 season Chelsea finished in third place in the Premier League. However, as the European competition was growing it meant that an extra place was granted to some countries which allowed the Blues to enter the tournament at the third qualifying round.

Albeit 44 years after Chelsea should have competed in the European Cup they were now part of the continents elite competition, joining Man Utd and Arsenal as the country's representatives. This meant the Blues would need to bolster their squad to ensure they kept pace in all competitions domestically and abroad. They signed Gabriele Ambrosetti, Carlo Cudicini, Mario Melchiot and World Cup winner Didier Deschamps. However, the biggest move was for the Blackburn and England striker Chris Sutton for a club record £10m. He had won the league with Rovers and competed in the Champions League alongside former Chelsea youth product Graeme Le Saux.

Gianluca Vialli's men were drawn against Skonto Riga from Latvia in the third qualification round. The first leg (and the club's first ever match in the Champions League) was played at Stamford Bridge. They had just beaten Sunderland 4-0 in the Premier League at the weekend where Gus Poyet scored a wonder volley from Gianfranco Zola's assist.

The match started with Chelsea attacking the Matthew Harding end. The small crowd of 22,000 watched a piece of the club's history. They only had to wait half an hour for the first action. Dennis Wise was waiting to take a corner when Skonto's Andrejs Tereskinas kicked Frank Leboeuf off the ball and was given a red card. It wasn't until twenty minutes to go that the Blues took the lead through an unlikely scorer. It was the substitute, Celestine Babayaro, who netted from the edge of the box in front of the Shed End just ten minutes after coming on for Didier Deschamps. Poyet made it 2-0 a minute later before Sutton made it 3-0.

The second leg was goalless meaning that Chelsea qualified for the main competition and were drawn against Galatasaray from Turkey, Hertha Berlin from Germany and European giants AC Milan from Italy in group H.

GAME 71
Oh, Dennis Wise

AC Milan 1 Chelsea 1
26th October 1999

UEFA Champions League Group Stage Match 5

San Siro

Chelsea; Ed De Goey, Dan Petrescu (Jody Morris 46), Celestine Babayaro, Frank Leboeuf, Marcel Desailly, Didier Deschamps, Gus Poyet (Roberto Di Matteo 75), Dennis Wise, Albert Ferrer, Tore Andre Flo, Gianfranco Zola (Gabriele Ambrosetti 81)

Scorer; Wise

Booked; Ferrer, Zola

Manager; Gianluca Vialli

Referee; Nicolai Levnikov

Attendance; 74,855

In 1999 Chelsea had players from all around the world but had a strong connection with Italy. Six of the players were Italian including Roberto Di Matteo, Gianfranco Zola, Carlo Cudicini, Gabriele Ambrosetti, Sam Dalla Bona and Luca Percassi. Manager Gianluca Vialli also represented the Azzurri over 50 times. In addition, Dan Petrescu, Didier Deschamps, assistant manager Ray Wilkins and Marcel Desailly (signed from AC Milan) had played in Italy. Therefore, it was only fitting that they would be involved in an Anglo-Italian match-up in their first proper Champions League game.

The Milan side included players like Andriy Shevchenko, Paolo Maldini and Alessandro Costacurta. In the early 90s the Italian side appeared in three consecutive Champions League finals. They were favourites to beat Chelsea and were welcomed to Stamford Bridge for a much anticipated game between Chelsea and one of Europe's elite clubs.

A crowd of 33,000 turned up and saw the Blues hold their own. Zola hit the post for his side midway through the second half. This was the best chance of the game which ended 0-0 in Milan's 200th European match (compared to Chelsea's 62nd). The Blues then lost 2-1 at Hertha Berlin, beat Galatasaray both home and away before heading to the San Siro for another game against Milan.

Just like the game at Stamford Bridge the only Englishman that started the match was Chelsea captain Dennis Wise. He had scored in the previous Champions League fixture; a 5-0 thrashing at Galatasaray (which itself was memorable for the 'welcome' the Turkish fans had given the Blues). Wise was able to dominate the midfield creating many chances throughout the game.

There were around 15 minutes left to play and if the Blues could hold on to a draw they would only need a point from their last game at home to Hertha Berlin to secure progress to the next stage. Things looked good when Wise crossed from the right and his ball met the head of Gustavo Poyet and was only denied by Christian Abbiati in the Milan goal. Many travelling fans were on their feet but not for long because the Italian side went up the other end and took the lead through Oliver Bierhoff's header.

Chelsea didin't give up and sent on Roberto Di Matteo for Poyet. Di Matteo had not played in over a month but it didn't show. Within two minutes of coming on he received the ball just past the halfway line. His long through ball caught out the usually highly organised Milan defence to find the run of Wise. The captain showed amazing control as he neatly cushioned the ball on the edge of the box with his right foot before stroking the ball through the oncoming Abbiati's legs with his left foot to make the score 1-1. This is the game and the goal that inspired the Dennis Wise song that is still sung at Stamford Bridge today. It will go down as one of the most iconic goals in the club's history.

The game ended 1-1 and Vialli's men managed to beat Hertha Berlin in the next game to ensure they were part of the draw for the next group stage. They were joined by Feyenoord (Holland), Marseille (France) and Lazio from Italy. The Blues were able to steer their way into second place after the six games to face Barcelona in the quarter finals. Chelsea took the Spanish side to their limit and were only beaten by Barcelona after extra time. The Blues took a 3-1 lead to the Nou Camp (after being 3-0 up) only to lose 5-1. The Catalan side included Pep Guardiola, Luis Figo, Rivaldo, Patrick Kluivert, Bolo Zenden, Frank De Boer and Carlos Puyol. The Blues had more than held their own against some of the top sides in European football but had to wait until 2003 to test themselves in the Champions League again.

GAME 72
A non-British affair

Southampton 1 Chelsea 2
26th December 1999

Premier League

The Dell

Chelsea; Ed De Goey, Dan Petrescu (Jody Morris 87), Celestine Babayaro, Frank Leboeuf, Didier Deschamps, Gus Poyet, Roberto Di Matteo, Albert Ferrer, Gabriele Ambrosetti (Jon Harley 74), Tore Andre Flo, Emerson Thome

Scorer; Flo (2)

Booked; Babayaro, Deschamps, Ferrer, Leboeuf

Manager; Gianluca Vialli

Referee; Paul E Alcock

Attendance; 15,232

Boxing Day football has always been a tradition for many generations. Gone are the days when teams would play on Christmas day and then travel to play the same team the next day. The last time Chelsea played on Christmas Day was against Blackburn in 1958 with the Blues winning 3-0 at Ewood Park. However, 41 years later a fixture played at The Dell on Boxing Day set a precedent that is almost accepted without notable mention or surprise.

After recent wins in domestic and European competition as well as participation in the Champions League Chelsea were able to attract more high profile players, including those from abroad. Also, a number of other factors such as the removal of three foreigners rule meant there was a much larger pool for teams to pick from worldwide. The Blues boasted a number of international players including players from three different continents.

In the 1999/00 season Chelsea travelled to Southampton for a repeat of the

169

previous year's Boxing Day fixture. However, Gianluca Vialli was without some key players including Dennis Wise and Gianfranco Zola through illness. Also, Marcel Desailly and Jes Hogh were both unavailable through injury. This did allow their new Brazilian defender, Emerson Thome, to deputise in the heart of the defence. He became the first Brazilian to play for the club.

The starting line up for Chelsea was Ed de Goey (Holland), Dan Petrescu (Romania), Celestine Babayaro (Nigeria), Frank Leboeuf (France), Didier Deschamps (France), Gus Poyet (Uruguay), Roberto Di Matteo (Italy), Albert Ferrer (Spain), Gabriele Ambrosetti (Italy), Tore Andre Flo (Norway) and Emerson Thome (Brazil). What made this team memorable was that it was the first time in English football history that the entire team consisted entirely of overseas players.

It was the Norwegian striker Flo who netted both Chelsea goals in the 2-1 win. The Blues took a 2-0 lead into half time before Kevin Davies got one back for the Saints with ten minutes to play. The game did not finish with 11 overseas players as Englishmen Jody Morris and Jon Harley replaced Dan Petrescu and Gabriele Ambrosetti respectively. After the game the Blues manager defended his decision on his team selection and stated that it makes no difference as long as they speak the same language on the pitch.

In the following game there was another all overseas starting XI but it was Morris who will go down in the record books as the player that scored the last Premier League goal before Y2K.

GAME 73

Bash at the beach

Chelsea 4 Charlton Athletic 1
11th January 2003

Premier League

Stamford Bridge

Chelsea; Carlo Cudicini, Celestine Babayaro, Marcel Desailly, Frank Lampard, Jimmy Floyd Hasselbaink, William Gallas, Graeme Le Saux (Gianfranco Zola 78), Emmanuel Petit, Eidur Gudjohnsen, John Terry (Jody Morris 22), Jesper Gronkjaer (Boudewijn Zenden 81)

Scorers; Hasselbaink, Gallas, Gudjohnsen, Le Saux

Booked; Le Saux, Desailly, Petit, Gudjohnsen

Manager; Claudio Ranieri

Referee; Mike L Dean

Attendance; 37,284

Premier League pitches are almost like carpets nowadays. They are tended to all year round with artificial light, regular watering, undersoil heating as well as a dedicated team of grounds staff to tend to the pitch. This has been so important to ensure that scheduled matches happen when they are meant to due to the globalisation of the game as well as not disappointing matchday going supporters.

In the 1980s four English clubs, including West London rivals QPR, installed 'astro-turf' pitches to stop adverse weather affecting games being postponed. The concept may have been a good idea but it was apparent that in real life it wasn't ideal. Players complained of injuries, carpet burns and even mentioned that the ball did not bounce true. These types of pitches were later banned from English league football.

In 2003 Chelsea hosted a Premier League game against Charlton Athletic. Referee Mike Dean inspected the pitch before the game and had doubts about whether the game should go ahead. There was not a lot of grass on the pitch but did have plenty of sand. It was not the most ideal surface to play on but Dean agreed for the match to go ahead.

The 'pitch' may have been a contributing factor to the game, especially in the third minute when Chelsea striker Jimmy Floyd Hasselbaink was brought down in the area by Charlton's Chris Powell. The Dutchman converted the penalty. Less than ten minutes later Powell was at fault again and William Gallas, who was standing in for the injured Mario Melchiot, fired in a volley past Dean Kiely. With just over half an hour played Eidur Gudjohnsen made it 3-0. Charlton did get a goal back from the penalty spot when Jason Euell slotted the ball past Ed De Goey after Marcel Desailly had been penalised for holding back Kevin Lisbie. Graeme Le Saux made it 4-1 in the second half to give Chelsea all three points.

After the game Charlton manager Alan Curbishley did not blame the pitch for his team's performance. However, the club's Chief Executive, Peter Varney, put in a formal request for the game to be replayed as he believed the playing surface was a breach of Premier League rules. He argued that it was more like an artificial surface and had his club been given notice they could have prepared better for the game. His appeal was turned down and the result stood.

Straight after the final whistle the pitch, or beach as it was often referred as, had diggers sent on to prepare the work needed for re-turfing. The Blues were fined £5,000 for the state of the pitch and another £3,000 for failing to tell Charlton about it.

GAME 74
Turmoil, tension and transition

Chelsea 2 Liverpool 1
11th May 2003

Premier League
Stamford Bridge
Chelsea; Carlo Cudicini, Celestine Babayaro, Marcel Desailly, Frank Lampard, Jimmy Floyd Hasselbaink (Carlton Cole 80), William Gallas, Graeme Le Saux, Mario Melchiot, Emmanuel Petit, Eidur Gudjohnsen (Gianfranco Zola 72), Jesper Gronkjaer (Mario Stanic 68)
Scorers; Desailly, Gronkjaer
Booked; Gallas, Hasselbaink, Le Saux
Manager; Claudio Ranieri
Referee; Alan G Wiley
Attendance; 41,911

The 2002/03 season was one of the most important in the Blues history. Chelsea said goodbye to several players including Roberto Di Matteo (retired through injury), Mikael Forssell, Mark Bosnich, Sam Dalla Bona and Slavisa Jokanovic. The only signing they made was the uncapped Spanish midfielder Enrique De Lucas from Espanyol as a free transfer. The Blues had many great players left in their squad including Frank Lampard, John Terry, Marcel Desailly, Jimmy Floyd Hasselbaink, Eidur Gudjohnsen, Jesper Gronkjaer and Gianfranco Zola.

It would be a season set to include turmoil, tension and transition. What was not known to many Chelsea fans was the financial difficulty the club had run into. Despite recent successes on the pitch there were less in the boardroom.

On the final day of the league campaign Chelsea welcomed Liverpool to Stamford Bridge. Both clubs were fighting it out for the last remaining Champions League place and was dubbed the £20m match. The money meant a lot to the Chelsea board. In fact, chief executive Trevor Birch even went into the home dressing room before kick off to say that if they failed to qualify there would be drastic cost-cutting including the wage bill for many top players.

Things did not start well for the Blues when Sami Hyypia opened the scoring for the Merseysiders after 11 minutes. Whether it was Birch's words before the game, the team spirit on the pitch or the willingness of the crowd it didn't take long for Chelsea to be level. Three minutes later Jesper Gronkjaer put in a cross that was headed in from Desailly past Jerzy Dudek. If the home side avoided defeat then they would claim the remaining Champions League place.

Just before the half hour mark came one of the most memorable Chelsea goals of all time. Gronkjaer received the ball out wide on the right hand side. He took on Liverpool defender John Arne Riise, cutting inside and hit a curling left foot shot into the Liverpool net. The crowd erupted, players celebrated and the Chelsea board probably quietly wiped their sweaty brow. Liverpool's Steven Gerrard was sent off towards the end of the game after a receiving a second yellow card.

Before the match Blues legend Gianfranco Zola announced that he would be leaving Stamford Bridge to return to Italy and had agreed to join Cagliari, from his native Sardinia. One of his last contributions in a Chelsea shirt really summed up his time at the club. He had the ball near the corner flag and was pressured by Liverpool defender Jamie Carragher. Zola toyed with him and left Carragher on his backside. He did get up and was then supported by a fellow team mate. The Italian maestro then danced his way past both men and left Carragher on the floor again! Danny Murphy then came to challenge Zola but he easily jinked inside. Eventually 'Franco was crowded out and the ball went out for a goal kick.

Chelsea managed to hold on to their 2-1 lead to gain the qualification they so badly needed. Although it was dubbed as a £20m game, it could be considered that it was worth £1bn! Russian Oligarch Roman Abramovich was interested in investing in an English football club. There were rumours that he was looking at Tottenham Hotspur but was finally convinced to buy Chelsea Football Club. Shortly after the season finished Abramovich paid chairman Ken Bates £140m for the club. One of his first jobs was to try to convince Gianfranco Zola to stay. However, the Italian was a man of his word and decided to play for Cagliari in Serie B. Although it has not been officially confirmed by Chelsea the number 25 shirt, as worn by Zola, has since been retired.

Some people will say this is the most important game in Chelsea history, others will have their own ideas but none will disagree that this was and still is one of the most memorable games in the Blues history.

GAME 75
The Roman era

MSK Zilina 0 Chelsea 2
13th August 2003

UEFA Champions League Preliminary Round (1st Leg)
Stadium Pod Dubnom
Chelsea; Carlo Cudicini, Glen Johnson, Marcel Desailly, Frank Lampard, Damien Duff (Joe Cole 70), Geremi, Wayne Bridge, Juan Sebastian Veron, Eidur Gudjohnsen, John Terry, Mikael Forssell (Jesper Gronkjaer 57)
Scorers; Gudjohnsen, Drahno (O.G)
Manager; Claudio Ranieri
Referee; Rene Temmink
Attendance; 6,160

The summer of 2003 was probably the most exciting in Chelsea history. Russian billionaire Roman Abramovich had just bought the club and was more than happy to splash the cash. He wanted to turn the Blues into a major force in world football, starting with recruitment to the playing side and training facilities. Little was known about the new owner, especially as he refused to talk to the media.

Although fans and the media were excited to see exactly what Abramovich would do with his money it did send the playing and coaching staff into a period of uncertainty. Gianfranco Zola knew he was already leaving the club and was joined by Albert Ferrer, Jody Morris, Graeme Le Saux and Ed De Goey as other transfers out of the club. The question was who could Chelsea and their new money attract. By the end of the summer transfer window they had signed Hernan Crespo, Claude Makelele, Damien Duff, Joe Cole, Juan Sebastian Veron, Adrian Mutu, Wayne Bridge, Geremi and Glen Johnson amongst a few others who cost a total of around £110m!

These new signings were welcomed into the club by manager Claudio Ranieiri who had been trusted to continue leading this team to glory. His side already included Frank Lampard, John Terry, Marcel Desailly, Carlo Cudicini, Jimmy Floyd Hasselbaink and Eidur Gudjohnsen. There was no doubt that the Blues had a squad to compete on all levels.

The first game of the Roman Abramovich was a Champions League preliminary round match against MSK Zilina from Slovakia. The first leg was played at Pod Dubnom in front of a crowd of 6,160. Six of the summer signings made their Chelsea debuts; Johnson, Duff, Geremi, Bridge and Veron. Joe Cole played his first game after he replaced Duff in the second half.

Chelsea took the lead towards the end of the first half. Damien Duff received the ball in his own half and dribbled forward. After taking on one Zilina player he played it neatly to Mikael Forssell who then gave it back before laying it off for Eidur Gudjohnsen. The Icelandic striker netted from close range past Ivan Trabalik to go 1-0 up.

The Blues, or rather Zilina, made it 2-0 in the second half. Chelsea were cruising and were looking to double their lead. Gudjohnsen tried to latch on to a through ball but was quickly dispossessed by the Slovakian, Michal Drahno but his interception flew past his own goalkeeper from just inside the penalty area.

In the return leg at Stamford Bridge the Blues won 3-0 with goals from Glen Johnson, Robert Huth and Jimmy Floyd Hasselbaink. The 5-0 aggregate win was more than enough to ensure they would be entered into the group stage of the Champions League where they were joined in group G by Sparta Prague, Besiktas and Lazio.

GAME 76
Happy birthday hattrick

Chelsea 5 Wolves 2
27th March 2004

Premier League

Stamford Bridge

Chelsea; Marco Ambrosio, Celestine Babayaro, Claude Makelele, Frank Lampard, Joe Cole (Scott Parker 80), William Gallas, Geremi (Jimmy Floyd Hasselbaink 60), Mario Melchiot, Hernan Crespo, Eidur Gudjohnsen (Damien Duff 45), John Terry

Scorers; Hasselbaink (3), Melchiot, Lampard

Manager; Claudio Ranieri

Referee; Graham P Barber

Attendance; 41,215

It's hard to know what you should get a professional footballer for their birthday, especially with the amount of money they earn where they can buy what they want, when they want. However, all players really want to do is play football. Back in Chelsea's maiden season Jimmy Windridge became the first person to play for the club on his birthday. Six years later Sam Downing was the first to score on his birthday in a 2-0 FA Cup win vs Leyton.

Fast forward to March 2004 and Chelsea were second in the Premier League, chasing the undefeated leaders Arsenal. They welcomed Wolverhampton Wanderers to Stamford Bridge. Earlier in the season the Blues had won 5-0 at Molineux which included two goals from super sub Hernan Crespo. One player who was hoping to start the home game was striker Jimmy Floyd Hasselbaink as it was his birthday. Sadly for him, manager Claudio Ranieri had placed the Dutchman on the bench.

Mario Melchiot gave Chelsea the lead as early as the fourth minute but Wolves, sitting bottom of the table, were not going to roll over. In fact they drew level later in the first half through Henri Camara. With the scores level at half time Ranieri decided to make a substitution. The Icelandic striker Eidur Gudjohnsen was replaced by Damien Duff, not Hasselbaink. Wolves then took a shock lead in the 57th minute when Jody Craddock headed home from a corner past Marco Ambrosio at the Shed End.

Now it was time for another Chelsea change and this time it was the birthday boy, Jimmy Floyd Hasselbaink. In the 60th minute the striker replaced Geremi and within ten minutes Frank Lampard had levelled the score.

With fifteen minutes to go Hasselbaink had struck a shot from 25 yards out that beat Paul Jones in the Wolves goal. This made him only the second player to score on his birthday as a sub, with Tommy Langley the other back in 1975 vs Birmingham. Chelsea now had a 3-2 lead. To make things even better he equalled a feat only ever achieved by Eric Oakton in 1935 and John Spencer in 1995 by scoring twice on his birthday, with three minutes to go. However, he wasn't finished there and in the final minute of the match he completed his hattrick.

Not only had Jimmy Floyd Hasselbaink become a member of the birthday goalscorers club he did it with style. He was the first person to bag a hattrick on his special day. Also no other person had ever scored three goals in a game as a sub. All of this in just half an hour. Chelsea won 5-2 on the day but will be remembered fondly by Hasselbaink for years to come.

GAME 77
Making a noise at the library

Arsenal 1 Chelsea 2
6th April 2004

UEFA Champions League Quarter-Final (2nd leg)
Highbury
Chelsea; Marco Ambrosio, Claude Makelele, Frank Lampard, Jimmy Floyd Hasselbaink (Hernan Crespo 82), Damien Duff (Joe Cole 82), William Gallas, Mario Melchiot, Wayne Bridge, Scott Parker (Jesper Gronkjaer 45), Eidur Gudjohnsen, John Terry
Scorers; Lampard, Bridge
Booked; Gallas, Hasselbaink, Cole
Manager; Claudio Ranieri
Referee; Markus Merk
Attendance; 35,486

Chelsea were enjoying their time under new ownership. Not only were they challenging for the league title but they were reaching the latter stages of cup competitions. In the FA Cup and League Cup they got to the fifth round. However, it was the Champions League that most fans had their eye on.

In the 2002/03 season the Blues were eliminated from the UEFA Cup in the first round by Viking FK Stavanger. This could have been a complete shock to lose to the Norwegian side, but in the two previous seasons they had been eliminated in the first and second rounds to other European minnows. In the 2003/04 season Chelsea found themselves upgraded into the Champions League.

After getting through the qualifying rounds the Blues were drawn in a group with Lazio, Besiktas and Sparta Prague. It was a relatively painless group stage with Claudio Ranieri's men winning four of their games and finishing top of the group. In the first knockout round they earned a trip to Germany to face Stuttgart. It was a very low scoring tie with the only goal that separated the sides was an own goal by Stuttgart's Fernando Meira. Chelsea's reward was an all-English quarter final vs London rivals, Arsenal.

Arsenal were top of the league when they faced the Blues and went on to win the league. Remarkably they did it without losing a single game and were labelled the 'Invincibles'. They were favourites to progress into the semi-final and this was further strengthened after the first leg. Despite Eidur Gudjohnsen giving Chelsea the lead at Stamford Bridge it only lasted six minutes until Robert Pires equalised. With ten minutes to go the Blues captain, Marcel Desailly, was given a yellow card and within five minutes he was sent off for a second bookable offence. This meant he would miss the return leg at Highbury.

Ranieri's men travelled to North London for a tense showdown at Highbury. The game could have gone either way but on the stroke of half time Jose Antonio Reyes gave the Gooners the lead from close range. During the interval the Chelsea boss made one change with Jesper Gronkjaer coming on to replace Scott Parker.

Six minutes into the second half saw Chelsea on the attack. A surprising effort from defensive midfielder Claude Makelele was only parried by Jens Lehman before Frank Lampard pounced to get an equaliser. The aggregate score now stood at 2-2 with both teams getting an away goal. As time went on it looked as though the game would head into extra time.

With only a few minutes left on the clock Wayne Bridge brought the ball forward into the Arsenal half. He remained unchallenged and was able to pick out Gudjohnsen in the box. Bridge carried on his run into the penalty area and received a pass back from his Icelandic teammate. A first time left-footed strike flew past Lehman and into the Arsenal net. Wayne Bridge had done it! The Chelsea fans, players and staff went mad with excitement. They had turned the Highbury library into a cauldron of noise, or at least one section of the ground. If Arsene Wenger's men were to qualify they would need two goals in the final few minutes due to Bridge's strike being an away goal. It didn't happen and the Blues were now into a Champions League semi final against Monaco.

Unfortunately for Chelsea a 3-1 defeat at the Stade Louis was too much to overturn. Monaco even had a man sent off with forty minutes left to play but in that time they managed to score twice without reply. In the return leg at Stamford Bridge the Blues went 2-0 up before conceding twice, losing 5-3 on aggregate. These matches gave Ranieri the nickname 'The Tinkerman' due to some of the changes he made and the result was probably enough for the board to look for a new manager straight after this.

GAME 78
The Special One

Chelsea 1 Man Utd 0
15th August 2004

Premier League
Stamford Bridge
Chelsea; Petr Cech, Claude Makelele, Alexey Smertin, Frank Lampard, William Gallas, Geremi (Ricardo Carvalho 89), Didier Drogba (Mateja Kezman 70), Wayne Bridge, Paulo Ferreira, Eidur Gudjohnsen (Scott Parker 82), John Terry
Scorer; Gudjihnsen
Manager; Jose Mourinho
Referee; Graham Poll
Attendance; 41,483

Just like the previous summer the money spent by Chelsea in the transfer window showed their commitment to compete for the biggest titles. The Blues spent big on Didier Drogba, Petr Cech, Arjen Robben, Tiago and Mateja Kezman. In addition there was a raid on Porto with Paulo Ferreira and Ricardo Carvalho strengthening the Chelsea defence. However, it was not a player who caused the biggest stir amongst the football world. It was their new manager, Jose Mourinho.

Mourinho had guided Porto to Champions League glory at the end of last season beating Monaco in the final, the team that knocked Chelsea out in the semis. The Portuguese boss first came to English media attention when his side knocked out Man Utd in the first knockout round. When Porto took a 3-2 aggregate lead with ten minutes to go, Jose left his seat in the technical area and ran down to the corner flag to celebrate with his players. This did not impress the Utd manager, Sir Alex Ferguson.

In June 2004 Chelsea announced they would have a new manager after the sacking of Claudio Ranieri. It was none other than Jose Mourinho. His first press conference is still talked about to this day where he declared himself 'a special one' and 'not from the bottle' in terms of his credentials for taking the Blues to the next level.

During the summer they had taken part in a tour of America prior to heading back to Stamford Bridge for a final friendly before the season started. It was the Gianfranco Zola tribute match where they ran out 3-0 winners. It was only six days until the first competitive game, a match up with title rivals Man Utd.

There was always going to be a lot of hype surrounding Jose Mourinho's first game in charge. Not only had he just won the Champions League and spent almost £100m but it was a rematch against Sir Alex Ferguson.

Although the game itself was not a classic it did give debuts to Petr Cech, Alexey Smertin, Ricardo Carvalho, Mateja Kezman, Paulo Ferreira and Didier Drogba. However, it was Eidur Gudjohnsen who grabbed the headlines as he scored the only goal of the game after 15 minutes to get the upperhand over their title rivals. The rest of the season was a joy to watch and there was rarely a day that the new Chelsea boss was not written about in most newspapers.

GAME 79
The greatest game of football

Chelsea 4 Barcelona 2
8th March 2005

UEFA Champions League Round 1 (2nd Leg)
Stamford Bridge
Chelsea; Petr Cech, Claude Makelele, Ricardo Carvalho, Frank Lampard, Mateja Kezman, Joe Cole, Damien Duff (Robert Huth 85), William Gallas, Paulo Ferreira (Glen Johnson 51), Eidur Gudjohnsen (Tiago 78), John Terry
Scorers; Gudjohnsen, Lampard, Duff, Terry
Booked; Ferreira, Kezman, Johnson
Manager; Jose Mourinho
Referee; Pierluigi Collina
Attendance; 41,515

In 2005 the world of football was dominated by Barcelona and one man in particular. The Brazilian striker Ronaldinho began to make a name for himself when he scored a 40 yard freekick against England at the 2002 World Cup. His performances made Barcelona turn their interests to him and he transferred from PSG in 2003.

In Jose Mourinho's first season as Chelsea manager he easily navigated his side through the group stage finishing top and progressing alongside his former club, Porto. Barcelona only managed to finish second despite a squad that included Ronaldinho, Samuel Eto'o, Deco, Andres Iniesta, Xavi and a Lionel Messi who had just been promoted from their youth set up.

In the knockout stage the Blues and the Catalan club were drawn against each other. At the time of the draw the two clubs were probably the most talked abouts sides in Europe due to their style of play, attacking prowess and the money they could both spend. As Chelsea had won their group they were given home advantage in the second leg meaning a trip to the Nou Camp would be up first.

In the Champions League pre-match build up Jose Mourinho was at a press conference and famously announced both starting line ups including the referee. He only made one mistake. He named Eidur Gudjohnsen in his starting line-up but on the night he was on the bench with Damien Duff taking his place.

The first leg was played in front of almost 90,000 people and they witnessed drama and controversy. Much to the home side's surprise it was Chelsea who took the lead. After 32 minutes future blue Juliano Belletti scored an own goal after deflecting Damien Duff's cross. Ronaldinho and his men pressed for an equaliser but the visitors would not budge before half time.

In the second half Chelsea striker Didier Drogba was sent off for an innocuous challenge on Victor Valdes in the Barcelona goal. Referee Anders Frisk gave the Ivorian a red card despite protests from the player. Fifteen minutes later Barca used their extra man advantage when substitute Maxi Lopez equalised. More woe was yet to come when another future blue, Samuel Eto'o, scored a winner for the home side. Chelsea boss Mourinho accused the referee of entering the Barcelona dressing room at half time to talk to manager Frank Rijkaard. This turned out to be false but did not stop UEFA giving Mourinho a two-game touchline ban should they reach the quarter final. However, Frisk had decided to quit refereeing after this match due to rumoured death threats he received from fans.

In Chelsea's next game they beat Liverpool in the 2005 League Cup final. It was the first trophy under Jose Mourinho but they wanted something bigger with the Premier League and Champions League still available to win.

The anticipation before the game was huge. This was potentially the greatest game of football seen at Stamford Bridge for a long time. On the 8th of March 2005 the Chelsea fans in attendance and around the world were not disappointed. Even neutrals would marvel at what would unfold in the next 90 minutes.

It was the Blues who took an early lead when Eidur Gudjohnsen scored in front of the Shed after just eight minutes. Frank Lampard then doubled their lead ten minutes later before Duff made it 3-0 inside 20 minutes. Chelsea were in dream land and Barca didn't know what had hit them. However, just before the half hour mark a ball was lobbed into the Chelsea penalty area and it was judged to have hit Paulo Ferreira on the hand. Pierluigi Collina, who had been appointed the referee after Frisk's decision to quit, pointed to the spot and Ronaldinho made no mistake from 12 yards.

With half time fast approaching the Blues were still in control of their own destiny until a moment of magic from Ronaldinho surprised everybody in the ground. He received the ball on the edge of the 18 yard box with seemingly nowhere to go. A couple of hip swivels on the spot and a toe poked effort flew into Petr Cech's net. There was a stunned silence from the crowd. Chelsea were now behind in the tie due to the away goals rule.

The game could have gone either way with both teams coming close to scoring again. However, with fifteen minutes left the home side won a corner that was taken by Damien Duff. In a moment when you needed a leader to step up his game, the captain John Terry headed home from around the penalty spot. His goal nestled into Valdes' goal, although Ricardo Carvalho may have had a bit of a hand in the goal going in. It didn't matter, Chelsea were back in front.

In the dying minutes of the game Barcelona were denied by Petr Cech to ensure that the Blues would progress into the quarter final. It was truly a game of great magic, atmosphere, drama and brilliance. The up and coming rising stars of world football had beaten one of the European giants.

GAME 80
Premier League champions

Bolton 0 Chelsea 2
30th April 2005

Premier League
Reebok Stadium
Chelsea; Petr Cech, Claude Makelele (Alexey Smertin 90), Ricardo Carvalho, Frank Lampard, William Gallas, Geremi, Didier Drogba (Robert Huth 65), Eidur Gudjohnsen (Joe Cole 85), John Terry, Jiri Jarosik, Tiago
Scorer; Lampard (2)
Booked; Makelele
Manager; Jose Mourinho
Referee; Steve W Dunn
Attendance; 27,653

Back in 1955 Chelsea won their first league title. Fast forward to 2005 and the Blues were looking to win their second championship 100 years after they were formed. They had started well, had been top since November and were setting records along the way. Jose Mourinho's men had managed ten consecutive clean sheets, winning all but one of those games.

It was the 23rd of April 1955 when Chelsea clinched their first league trophy and on the same date fifty years later the Blues beat neighbours Fulham 3-1 at Stamford Bridge with goals from Joe Cole, Frank Lampard and Eidur Gudjohnsen. The result put them 14 points clear of nearest rivals Arsenal. Two days later Arsenal played Tottenham in the North London derby knowing that Chelsea would be handed the Premier League crown without even kicking a ball if they failed to win. A first half goal from Jose Antonio Reyes was enough to ensure the Blues would still need to wait a little longer to become champions.

After the Fulham game came a Champions League semi final first leg against Liverpool at Stamford Bridge. It ended 0-0 and Mourinho's men could concentrate on the second leg after a league match against Bolton Wanderers at the Reebok Stadium.

On the 30th April 2005 the Blues travelled to Bolton for a late afternoon kick off. Arsenal hadn't played that day and so Chelsea's destiny was in their own hands. They knew that a win would guarantee that Roman Abramovich would have accomplished one of the things he set out to do when he bought the club.

In the tunnel John Terry was inspiring his team by telling them that this was their year. Bolton started the game well creating the better chances but Petr Cech was equal to all their efforts. Towards the end of the first half Chelsea captain John Terry was caught by a flailing arm and needed lengthy treatment on his eye. There were rumours at half time that he was suffering from impaired vision. Despite this JT carried on and played the entire game.

After an hour the ball was pumped into the Bolton half and flicked on by Eidur Gudjohnsen. Jiri Jarosik appeared to have fouled Fernando Hierro but it went unnoticed by the referee. Didier Drogba then headed the ball over the last line of defence for Frank Lampard to collect. Lamps headed the ball neatly down and cut inside with his left foot before unleashing a strike from 12 yards that flew past Jussi Jaaskelainen to make it 1-0 to Chelsea. He ran over to the visiting fans to celebrate and was joined by his team mates. Could that be the goal the sealed his team's first ever Premier League trophy?

With fifteen minutes to go Bolton won a corner and it was swung into the Chelsea penalty box. It was cleared out wide to Gudjohnsen who played it forward to Claude Makelele near the halfway line. His control, turn and vision helped pick out a pass to Lampard who was joined by Ricardo Carvalho on the counter attack. Lamps could have squared it to the Portuguese defender but instead he decided to coolly go round the Bolton keeper and knock the ball into an open net. At this point the Blues fans, players and staff were ecstatic. They knew they had done enough to win the title with three games left to play.

After the match the cameras focussed on the manager Jose Mourinho who was smiling whilst talking on his mobile phone. Rather than taking the limelight from the players he had rung his family to speak to them. However, the Chelsea fans and players knew that he was a main factor in turning these great players into champions of England and installed a winning mentality within the club. This then went on to breed more success and more silverware. This game was one of the most celebrated and memorable amongst Chelsea fans and the story will live on for generations to come.

GAME 81
Hunt, Head, Hospital and Helmet

Reading 0 Chelsea 1
14th October 2006

Premier League
Madejski Stadium
Chelsea; Petr Cech (Carlo Cudicini 5), Michael Essien, Andriy Shevchenko (Joe Cole 63), Frank Lampard, Khalid Boulahrouz, Didier Drogba, John Mikel Obi, Arjen Robben (Salomon Kalou 82), Wayne Bridge, Paulo Ferreira, John Terry
Scorer; Ingimarsson (O.G)
Sent off; Mikel
Booked; Mikel, Terry
Manager; Jose Mourinho
Referee; Mike A Riley
Attendance; 24,025

Chelsea were the current Premier League champions, winning it twice in as many seasons. In October 2006 the Blues travelled to newly promoted Reading. By this time Jose Mourinho's men included players like Michael Essien, Andriy Shevchenko and John Mikel Obi in addition to the spine of the last few years of Cech, Terry, Lampard and Drogba.

Chelsea won the game 1-0 through an own goal scored by Ivar Ingimarsson. Mikel was also sent off for a second bookable offence by referee Mike Riley. However, this is not what made the game memorable.

In the first 30 seconds of the game Khalid Boulahrouz was chasing back to stop Reading's Stephen Hunt from getting on the end of a through ball. Petr Cech came out to collect a ball in his penalty area but the Irish striker's knee connected with the Chelsea keeper in the head. Play was stopped for several minutes before the Czech international goalkeeper had to be stretchered off and taken to hospital. He later underwent surgery for a depressed skull fracture which nearly cost him his life. After this injury and a lengthy lay off Petr Cech began to wear special headgear for protection. Stephen Hunt was not even cautioned by the referee, Mike Riley.

Cech was replaced in goal by substitute keeper Carlo Cudicini. The Italian did well to stop Reading from scoring. The home side were quite aggressive in their style which led to a few yellow cards, most notably for defender Andre Bikey in the 76th minute. He had fouled Didier Drogba who was bursting forward from the halfway line. Just six minutes later Bikey fouled Drogba again and was sent off after coming on as a substitute.

In the last minute of the game Reading won a corner and it was crossed into the Chelsea penalty area but it was punched clear by Cudicini. However, he was fouled by Ibrahima Sonko, knocked unconscious and also needed to be carried off on a stretcher. The Italian goalkeeper was unable to continue and Mourinho had made all three substitutes. Even if he hadn't there was no third choice keeper on the bench. This meant that one of the outfield players would have to go in. That's when the Blues captain John Terry put on the goalkeepers gloves and shirt and played the remaining time in goal.

The game ended 1-0 in Chelsea's favour but it was not until the 20th January 2007 that Petr Cech was available to play in goal again. As for Cudicini, he didn't return until appearing on the bench vs Sheffield Utd two weeks after his injury. Henrique Hilario deputised in goal during that time and made his debut four days after the Reading game in a Champions League game against Barcelona at Stamford Bridge. Chelsea won 1-0 and he kept the jersey for five consecutive games. 20-year old Yves Makabu-Ma-Kalambay was on the bench as cover until Cudicini was back but was never used.

GAME 82
A win at the new Wembley

Chelsea 1 Man Utd 0
(After Extra Time)
19th May 2007

FA Cup Final
Wembley
Chelsea; Petr Cech, Claude Makelele, Michael Essien, Frank Lampard, Joe Cole (Arjen Robben 46 (Ashley Cole 108)), Didier Drogba, John Mikel Obi, Wayne Bridge, Paulo Ferreira, Shaun Wright-Phillips (Salomon Kalou 93), John Terry
Scorer; Drogba
Booked; Makelele, Kalou, A Cole, Ferreira
Manager; Jose Mourinho
Referee; Steve G Bennett
Attendance; 89,826

At the end of the 1999/00 season Chelsea won the last FA Cup final at the old Wembley Stadium. The Blues beat Aston Villa 1-0 via a Roberto Di Matteo goal. However, this was not the last domestic game to be played there. The Community Shield in 2000 saw Chelsea take on Premier League champions Man Utd. The reds were favourites to win the game but new signing Jimmy Floyd Hasselbaink scored on his debut and fellow Dutchman, Mario Melchiot, netted in a 2-0 win.

As Wembley Stadium was being redeveloped FA Cup finals were held at the Millennium Stadium in Cardiff, Wales. The Blues tasted FA Cup defeat against Arsenal in 2002 but did enjoy League Cup success vs Liverpool in 2005. However, in 2007 the new Wembley was to be re-opened and host the first FA Cup final in London for seven years. It was fitting that Chelsea, who played in the last Wembley FA Cup final, played against Man Utd.

Before the game started Prince William did the official opening, followed by a fly-past by the Red Arrows. Past winners of the FA Cup were paraded around the pitch including former Blues Ron Harris, Dennis Wise and Marcel Desailly.

The game started as a cagey affair with both sides being cautious and lacking creativity. At half time with the score 0-0 Chelsea manager Jose Mourinho brought on Arjen Robben for Joe Cole. However, the Dutchman was unable to break the deadlock and after 90 minutes the score remained goalless and extra time would be needed to find a winner for the third consecutive FA Cup final.

In extra time Man Utd believed they should have been awarded a goal. TV replays showed that Ryan Giggs' effort did cross the line but only after he had pushed Petr Cech into his own net. The referee, Steve Bennett, just waved play on. The game was heading for a penalty shootout until the 116th minute. Chelsea were on the attack and Didier Drogba played a neat one-two with Man of the Match, Frank Lampard, before prodding the ball past Edwin van der Sar.

The game ended 1-0. Not only had Didier Drogba, the King of Cup Finals, scored the first goal at the new Wembley, Chelsea were the first winners of the FA Cup in the new stadium. This was the first of four FA Cups that the Blues would win in six years.

GAME 83
Forget your history, we're going to Moscow

Chelsea 3 Liverpool 2
30th April 2008

UEFA Champions League Semi-Final (2nd Leg)

Stamford Bridge

Chelsea; Petr Cech, Ashley Cole, Claude Makelele, Michael Essien, Ricardo Carvalho, Frank Lampard (Andriy Shevchenko 119), Joe Cole (Nicolas Anelka 90), Didier Drogba, Michael Ballack, Salomon Kalou (Florent Malouda 70), John Terry

Scorers; Drogba (2), Lampard

Manager; Avram Grant

Referee; Roberto Rosetti

Attendance; 38,900

It was no secret that Chelsea owner Roman Abramovich was keen on winning the Champions League. In his first year with the club manager Claudio Ranieri guided them to the semi finals. A year later Jose Mourinho did the same, losing to Liverpool due to Luis Garcia's ghost goal. In the following season the Blues were drawn in the same group as Liverpool with both games ending 0-0. Chelsea qualified for the knockout stage but were dumped out by Barcelona.

In the 2006/07 season Chelsea again made it to the semi finals and again faced Liverpool. Joe Cole had given Mourinho's men a 1-0 lead in the first leg at Stamford Bridge. In the return game at Anfield it was Daniel Agger who made it 1-0 to the home side forcing the tie into extra time. No goals were scored and so penalties were needed to find a finalist. Liverpool won 4-1 on penalties with Arjen Robben and Geremi failing to score for the Blues.

Chelsea were so close to reaching their first Champions League final and the 2007/08 showpiece involved Abramovich's home country hosting it, in Moscow. In their opening game they faced Rosenborg from Norway. The Scandinavians surprised the Blues by earning a 1-1 draw and even took a 1-0 lead. Even more shocking was that manager Jose Mourinho was sacked after this game with the Director of Football, Avram Grant, taking over as boss. This made a lot of Chelsea fans upset and angry that the Special One was being replaced by someone without a decent track record.

Avram Grant's men did manage to get through the group stage before disposing Olympiacos and Fenerbahce. This then set up a semi final against... Liverpool. The two clubs had become fierce rivals due to the number of times they had played each other in recent history. Chelsea had been more dominant on the domestic front but Liverpool had the upperhand in Europe.

Just before the first leg Frank Lampard's mum was admitted into hospital for pneumonia. Frank had missed Premier League games against Wigan and Everton to be by her side. She appeared to be getting better so Lamps declared himself ready for the game vs Liverpool. It was the Merseysiders who looked like they had got the better of the Blues once more when Dirk Kuyt made it 1-0 just before half time. However, in the final minute of the game substitute Salomon Kalou crossed the ball from the left, it landed right on Riise's head. The Norwegian's stooped header flew past Pepe Reina into his own net to make a 1-1 on the night and is the reason why Chelsea fans love Salomon Kalou. After the game Lampard rushed back to hospital to be with his mum again.

Chelsea's next game was a title decider against Manchester Utd. A win for reds would mean the Blues would only be able to win the league via goal difference if results went their way. On the day the Blues did win 2-1 courtesy of two Michael Ballack goals, including one controversial penalty. Frank Lampard did not play because his mum had passed away two days earlier. The news of her death hit him hard.

For the second leg there was some uncertainty whether Lampard would play. In the end he declared himself ready and available to Avram Grant and the Israeli manager picked him from the start. Things began well when Didier Drogba opened the scoring after 33 minutes after smashing the ball home. It was enough to put them in front. In the second half, future blue, Fernando Torres equalised and at the end of 90 minutes the score was 1-1, with an aggregate score of 2-2; both teams scoring an away goal. This meant extra time was needed.

Michael Essien had the home fans jumping on their feet as his strike from the edge of the area flew into the Liverpool net. However, celebrations were cut short as it was ruled out for offside. A few minutes later they did have something to get excited about when Michael Ballack was tripped in the box by Liverpool's Sami Hyypia. The man to step up and take the penalty was Frank Lampard. It was a tense moment as players and fans watched on wondering if he was the right man for the job. There was no doubting his ability but his focus and concentration may have been compromised by the recent death of his mum.

Lampard steadied himself to take the spot kick and slotted it into the net with Pepe Reina diving the wrong way. The goalscorer then proceeded to run to the corner flag, got down on his knees and began to kiss his black armband, worn in memory of his mother. It was an emotional moment for him and for everybody associated with the club. He then sent a kiss to his dad who was watching in the stands.

There were still around twenty minutes to play but at the end of the first period of extra time the Ivorian striker put his team 3-1 up on the night. The whole ground erupted and fans could start planning their trip to Moscow. Ryan Babel had other ideas and his long range strike beat Petr Cech from 30 yards with just three minutes left. A goal for Liverpool would send them through to another Champions League final. Luckily for the Blues they managed to hold on and book their place in the final against fellow English club Manchester Utd.

GAME 84
Moscow misery

Chelsea 1 Man Utd 1
(After Extra Time. Score at 90 mins 1-1. Lost 5-6 on penalties)
21st May 2008

UEFA Champions League Final
Luzhniki Stadium
Chelsea; Petr Cech, Ashley Cole, Claude Makelele (Juliano Belletti 120), Michael Essien, Ricardo Carvalho, Frank Lampard, Joe Cole (Nicolas Anelka 99), Didier Drogba, Michael Ballack, Florent Malouda (Salomon Kalou 92), John Terry
Scorer; Lampard
Penalty Shoot-out; Ballack (scored), Belletti (scored), Lampard (scored), A Cole (scored), Terry (hit post), Kalou (scored), Anelka (saved)
Sent off; Drogba
Booked; Makelele, Carvalho, Ballack
Manager; Avram Grant
Referee; Lubos Michel
Attendance; 69,552

The stage was set for the first ever all-English Champions League final in Roman Abramovich's homeland of Russia. The road to Moscow had been pretty bumpy along the way but the Chelsea fans were excited by the club's first ever appearance in the final of Europe's greatest competition. Supporters had troubles trying to get flights, hotels, tickets and even visas (which were later not required if fans had a ticket for the game and a passport with at least six months left until expiration). Due to its location and time difference the game was not due to kick off until 22:45 local time, making it the only final that was played until the early hours of the next morning.

The Blues met Manchester Utd in the final. Both clubs had previously faced each other in a couple of FA Cup finals. In 2007 it was Didier Drogba who scored the only goal of the game at the new Wembley Stadium. However, in 1994 the 4-0 win for United was as miserable for Chelsea as was the weather. On the day of the Champions League final the weather was more like that of '94 so would the outcome be the same?

There were some unexpected selections for the final with central midfielder Michael Essien playing at right back rather than Paulo Ferreira in his natural position. Florent Malouda was preferred over Salomon Kalou. Also, left back Ashley Cole injured his right ankle in training the day before the match after a challenge with Claude Makelele. Luckily, it wasn't too bad and Cole was able to start.

The game began and was fairly even for the first 20 minutes until Makelele and Paul Scholes clashed in mid-air, resulting in the English midfielder leaving the field for treatment with a bloody nose. Five minutes later Man Utd took the lead when Cristiano Ronaldo headed past Petr Cech. Both teams continued to attack each other and both keepers kept the score at 1-0. Just before half time Essien hit a long range shot and it deflected off a couple of Utd defenders, wrong footing Edwin van der Sar. Frank Lampard had made a run from deep and his simple finish made things level going into the break.

The game ended 1-1 after 90 minutes and so another half an hour of extra time was needed to try to separate the two sides and decide a winner. In extra time Lampard hit the underside of the crossbar and John Terry headed Ryan Giggs' effort over the bar.

With just five minutes left to play Terry went down with cramp and the ball was put out of play to receive treatment. When the ball came back into play Utd's striker Carlos Tevez put the ball out for a throw deep in the Blues half and urged his teammates to put pressure on. This did not please the

Chelsea players and a huge melee occurred. During the tussle assistant referee Martin Balko reported that Didier Drogba had slapped Nemanja Vidic and was then sent off. He became only the second player to be sent off in a Champions League final.

After 120 minutes of football the score remained 1-1 and so penalties were needed to distinguish a winner. The United captain Rio Ferdinand won the toss and chose for his team to take the first kick in front of his own fans. Tevez 0-1, Ballack 1-1, Carrick 1-2, Belletti (who came on as a sub in the last minute) 2-2. Next up was Cristiano Ronaldo. He had already beaten Petr Cech once and looked to bury his penalty. He stuttered his run up but the Chelsea keeper was not fazed and the score remained 2-2! Lampard 3-2, Hargreaves 3-3, Ashley Cole 4-3.

Each team had one penalty left. Nani stepped up for Utd knowing that a miss would mean Chelsea would be crowned the Champions of Europe. However, the Portuguese attacker netted. This meant that if Chelsea's captain John Terry could score they would win. JT waited to take his spot kick and just before he hit it he slipped. He sent the ball to van der Sar's left with the tall Dutchman diving the wrong way. Fans could see this and a split second seemed to last a life time. Would the ball go in or would more penalties be needed. In the end Terry's kick was denied by the post.

Anderson made it 5-4 before Salomon Kalou scored his spot kick. Ryan Giggs netted to make it 6-5. Next up for Chelsea was French striker Nicolas Anelka. Unfortunately his poor attempt was saved by the Utd keeper denying the Blues from European glory and giving them plenty of heartache. After the game the players went to receive their runners up medal, with the exception of Didier Drogba who had been sent off and so not allowed to collect his. Chelsea manager Avram Grant took it on his behalf before throwing his own medal into the crowd. This would turn out to be Grant's last game in charge of the team before being sacked three days later.

GAME 85
It's a disgrace

Chelsea 1 Barcelona 1
6th May 2009

UEFA Champions League Semi-Final (2nd leg)
Stamford Bridge
Chelsea; Petr Cech, Ashley Cole, Michael Essien, Frank Lampard, Didier Drogba (Juliano Belletti 72), Michael Ballack, Florent Malouda, Jose Bosingwa, John Terry, Alex, Nicolas Anelka
Scorer; Essien
Booked; Essien, Alex, Ballack, Drogba
Manager; Guus Hiddink
Referee; Tom Henning Ovrebo
Attendance; 37,857

It was no secret that Chelsea owner Roman Abramovich had a desire to win the Champions League. The players shared his hunger after recent disappointments, including losing the final on penalties in the previous season to Man Utd. The board decided to make former World Cup winning manager Luiz Felipe Scolari their new boss. However, things didn't quite work out as planned and 'Big Phil' was dismissed in February 2009.

A couple of days after Scolari's sacking the club announced Russia's boss Guus Hiddink would take charge until the end of the season. Hiddink would also continue his work on the international stage at the same time. His appointment was welcomed by the players. Fans also began to embrace him, especially as what was becoming a yearly tradition saw the Blues play Liverpool in the Champions League with Chelsea winning 7-5 on aggregate. This set up a semi-final match up with Barcelona, starting at the Nou Camp.

The Blues travelled to Barca and left Spain with a 0-0 draw. It was a good result but Barcelona had a slight advantage as Chelsea were unable to score an away goal. A week later 41,000 people turned up to watch the semi-final second leg. A win for Chelsea would see a repeat of the previous year's final against Man Utd.

Referee Tom Henning Ovrebo from Norway blew his whistle to start the game. It was the home side who took the upperhand early on when Michael Essien scored one of the greatest ever goals at Stamford Bridge when his left-footed volley flew in past Victor Valdes from 25 yards.

Later on came refereeing controversy in a Chelsea/Baracelona game, and not for the first time. Florent Malouda was hauled down by Barcelona's Dani Alves in the box but Ovrebo denied the Blues a penalty and instead gave a freekick outside the box. Next up, Didier Drogba was tugged back by Eric Abidal but his claims were ignored. After this it was Drogba again who was appealing for a penalty after a challenge from Yaya Toure. Ovrebo did eventually send off Abidal in the second half before the Blues had a fourth penalty appeal turned down. Gerard Pique clearly handled the ball in the box with ten minutes left to play.

The biggest frustration came when a Michael Ballack volley hit the arm of Samuel Eto'o. Ovrebo shook his head and was chased by the German midfielder to express his anger at the decision. However, there was more disappointment when the Catalan's broke Chelsea hearts. In the final minute of the game Andres Iniesta scored making it 1-1 on the night and sent Barcelona into the final on the away goals rule. After the whistle Didier Drogba, who had been substituted with an injury, ran from the dugout to show his disgust. TV cameras picked up on the Ivorian striker and he spoke clearly down the lens about what a disgrace the refereeing was. The anger and injustice festered in fans hearts and minds for a long time. This match will always be remembered for the time the Blues were robbed by Ovrebo and UEFA-lona.

GAME 86
Against all odds

Barcelona 2 Chelsea 2
24th April 2012

UEFA Champions League Semi-Final (2nd leg)
Nou Camp

Chelsea; Petr Cech, Branislav Ivanovic, Ashley Cole, Ramires, Frank Lampard, Juan Mata (Salomon Kalou 58), Didier Drogba (Fernando Torres 80), John Mikel Obi, Raul Meireles, Gary Cahill (Jose Bosingwa 13), John Terry

Scorers; Ramires, Torres

Sent off; Terry

Booked; Mikel, Ramires, Ivanovic, Cech, Lampard, Meireles

Manager; Roberto Di Matteo

Referee; Cuneyt Cakir

Attendance; 95,845

Like many of the recent campaigns, Chelsea started the season wth a new manager. Andre Villas-Boas was an assistant under Jose Mourinho but had tried his own hand at management by taking on the vacant post at Academica in Portugal in 2009. His results and style of play attracted Porto and he became their boss the following summer. In his first season he won the Portguese Supercup and the league title without losing a single game. The next season he won the Portuguese Cup and the Europa League. At the age of 33 years old he had become the youngest ever manager to win a European competition. In the summer of 2011 he took up the managers position at Chelsea. He appointed former blue Roberto Di Matteo as his assistant.

His time at Chelsea started well in pre-season, winning all six games whilst conceding only once. He also began the Premier League confidently, only losing once in all competitions until a 1-0 loss to QPR in late October. In the Champions League he had guided Chelsea to the top of their group. They were then drawn against Napoli in the first knockout round. Things started well when Juan Mata gave the Blues a 1-0 lead at the San Paolo. However, the Italian side came back into the game before eventually winning the first leg 3-1. The return at Stamford Bridge was scheduled for three weeks later. However, Roman Abramovich had questioned some of AVB's team selections and after a 1-0 defeat to West Brom he was sacked.

By the time Napoli visited London Chelsea had given the managerial position to AVB's assistant, Roberto Di Matteo on a caretaker's responsibility until the end of the season. His team went 2-0 up through Didier Drogba and John Terry. Gokhan Inler got an important away goal for Napoli but a Frank Lampard penalty sent the game into extra time. Just before the end of the first period of extra time Branislav Ivanovic found himself high up the pitch and through some nice play around the box the ball fell kindly to Branna who smashed the ball home. The Blues had completed an unlikely comeback. They then swept past Benfica in the Quarter Finals before being drawn against Barcelona in the Semis.

Barcelona, with Messi, Iniesta, Xavi, Fabregas, Puyol and Pedro, came to Stamford Bridge for the first leg. A determined Chelsea side won the game 1-0 via a goal from Drogba at the end of the first half. The return leg at the Nou Camp a week later would be a tight affair. Barcelona had not scored an away goal but a trip to their huge stadium was an advantage.

Pep Guardiola's Barcelona side were feeling confident of progressing despite the 1-0 disadvantage. They had scored over 100 goals at the Nou Camp that season and they knew they had knocked the Blues out at the same stage a few years earlier.

Things did not start well for Chelsea as central defender Gary Cahill sustained an injury and was replaced by full back Jose Bosingwa after 13 minutes. Twenty minutes later Sergio Busquets gave the home side the lead on the night when his goal from a corner beat Petr Cech. Then came a moment of madness. Chelsea captain John Terry drove his knee into the back of Alexis Sanchez and was given a red card. This meant that the Blues were down to ten men, with no centre backs, against a team that had been labelled the greatest ever team in world football, and they were away from home. They seemed to have blown their chances, especially when Andres Iniesta scored just before halftime to make it 2-1 on aggregate.

However, many pundits, fans and probably Barcelona players doubted the Blues would recover but the Chelsea players did not give up. In the few remaining seconds of the first half the ball fell to Frank Lampard on the halfway line. His quick vision saw fellow midfielder Ramires making a run forward. Lamps through ball found the Brazilian who chipped the ball past Victor Valdes from the edge of the box. It was a superb finish and gave the Blues some hope of a comeback.

In the second half Barcelona continued to dominate the game and kept attacking an under strength Chelsea team. Three minutes after the restart Cesc Fabregas was brought down by the hero from the first leg, Didier Drogba. Referee Cuneyt Cakir didn't hesitate in pointing to the penalty spot despite the Ivorian pleading his innocence. Up stepped Lionel Messi to take the penalty. The Argentinian had won the Ballon D'Or every year since 2009. Petr Cech danced about on the line while waiting for Messi to take his penalty. Once he had struck the ball it hit the crossbar and flew out to safety. Chelsea had been let off but still had an uphill battle to qualify for the final in Munich.

Chelsea struggled on and were relieved when Barcelona had a goal disallowed for offside and Messi hit the post as well. In the final minute of the game the Catalan's were attacking the Chelsea goal when a shot was blocked, bounced around before being smashed clear by Jose Bosingwa.

The camera followed the ball. When it finally came back into shot it had fallen to the feet of Fernando Torres and he was heading towards Victor Valdes' goal. He was left one on one with the keeper who came rushing out to the edge of his box. The Chelsea striker neatly knocked the ball round him and stroked it into an empty net. Fans, players and even Gary Neville, who was commentating on the game, couldn't believe what they had just seen. From 2-0 down with ten men Chelsea had manage to get a 2-2 draw against the best team in the world at the Nou Camp. This meant they had a 3-2 aggregate win. It was too much for Pep Guardiola's side to overturn and so caretaker manager Roberto Di Matteo had taken his side to the Champions League final!

Although many fans were ecstatic with the result there was a slight blemish on the result. John Terry would miss the final through suspension. The same went for Raul Meireles, Ramires and Ivanovic. The Serbian was unaware of this until an after match interview with Geoff Shreeves. Branna just shrugged his shoulders and said "Oh well". Chelsea had been the underdogs and would be treated the same as they faced Bayern Munich in their own stadium in the final.

GAME 87
Champions of Europe

Chelsea 1 Bayern Munich 1
(After Extra Time. Score at 90 mins 1-1. Won 4-3 on penalties)
19th May 2012

UEFA Champions League Final

Allianz Arena

Chelsea; Petr Cech, Ashley Cole, David Luiz, Frank Lampard, Juan Mata, Didier Drogba, John Mikel Obi, Jose Bosingwa, Salomon Kalou (Fernando Torres 85), Gary Cahill, Ryan Bertrand (Florent Malouda 73)

Scorer; Drogba

Penalty Shoot-out; Mata (saved), Luiz (scored), Lampard (scored), Cole (scored), Drogba (scored)

Booked; Cole, Luiz, Drogba, Torres

Manager; Roberto Di Matteo

Referee; Pedro Proenca

Attendance; 69,901

Roberto Di Matteo had performed wonders after the sacking of Andre Villas-Boas. It was near impossible for him to mount a serious challenge for the league title so turned his attention to cup competitions. His first game as boss was an FA Cup fifth round replay against Birmingham at St Andrews. He saw second half goals from Juan Mata and Raul Meireles earn them a quarter final tie vs Leicester. Chelsea cruised to a 5-2 victory before beating Tottenham 5-1 at Wembley in the semis.

Chelsea took on Liverpool in the FA Cup final. Di Matteo was known to many football fans due to his Cup Final moments. In 1997 he scored after just 43 seconds as the Blues beat Middlesbrough 2-0, winning their first silverware in 26 years. A year later he scored in the League Cup final and in

2000 he scored the only goal in a 1-0 win against Aston Villa in the last FA Cup final at the old Wembley. It turned out that Robbie was a Wembley wizard as his side won 2-1 against Liverpool, with goals from Ramires and Didier Drogba before Andy Carroll's consolation goal.

Two weeks later Chelsea were in their second ever Champions League final. They were hoping to ease the heartache from the disappointment of losing the 2008 final in Moscow. However, they would have to do it without four key players who missed the game through suspension. Also, centre backs Gary Cahill and David Luiz had not played in a month. Bayern Munich were favourites as they had won their domestic title and were playing in their own city and own stadium. Their team included Manuel Neuer, Franck Ribery, Bastian Schweinsteiger, Mario Gomez, Thomas Muller, Philipp Lahm, Jerome Boateng, Toni Kroos and former blue Arjen Robben.

Chelsea had finished sixth in the Premier League meaning they would not qualify for next season's Champions League. Their only saving grace would be to win the trophy and be entered into the competition as champions. This would be at the expense of the fourth placed team, Tottenham. The pressure on Roberto Di Matteo and his side was immense.

Frank Lampard wore the captain's armband and led the team out on to the pitch. Portuguese referee Pedro Proenca blew his whistle and started the match. It was Bayern who started off well and dominated possession and shots at goal in the first half. They continued this into the second half and in the 83rd minute German striker Thomas Muller rose to head in a cross by Toni Kroos to break Chelsea hearts. After their heroics against Napoli and Barcelona there was little chance for the Blues to come back at this late stage.

With just a minute to go Chelsea won a corner. Juan Mata ran over to take it and his ball into the box was met by the Blues striker Didier Drogba. His powerful header was glanced past Neuer and then Di Matteo's men were level. Chelsea fans went wild and maybe, just maybe, they could carry the momentum into extra time. The referee blew his whistle and the game was level after 90 minutes, 1-1.

In extra time it was a case of lightning striking twice. The Blues hero Didier Drogba conceded a penalty, just like he did in the semi final against Barcelona. Things did not look good for Di Matteo's side. This time it was former Chelsea player Arjen Robben who would take the penalty. He confidently ran up but his strike was saved by Petr Cech. Somehow the Blues had escaped tradegy again. Surely it was their destiny to win the trophy.

No more goals were scored and so just like the 2008 final Chelsea would be involved in a penalty shootout to determine the winner. Munich went first and it was Lahm who put his side 1-0 up. Next up was Juan Mata but his spot kicked was saved by Manuel Neuer. Gomez then made it 2-0 to the Germans before David Luiz thumped his penalty into the goal. Goalkeeper Neuer took Bayern's third penalty and he converted it to make it 3-1.

Next up was captain Frank Lampard. He had scored in the 2008 shootout and it was the same outcome this time as he became only the second person in history to score in two European Cup final shootouts. Substitute Ivica Olic looked to make it 4-2 but his penalty was saved by Cech. If Ashley Cole could convert his spot kick the scores would be level at 3-3 with one penalty each left to take. Cole joined Lampard in the elite group of players to score in two shootouts.

Bayern Munich's fifth penalty was to be taken by Bastian Schweinsteiger. He looked focussed before stuttering on his run up. He was waiting for Cech to commit himself but the Czech shot-stopper did not move. It was enough to put the German off and he saw his penalty hit the post and away from the goal.

Just like the 2008 final the result was in their hands. Four years earlier John Terry had slipped whilst taking Chelsea's fifth penalty. This time JT was missing from the final but unlike the final in Moscow Didier Drogba was available to take one. The Ivorian was a huge character of the game and had already gained legend status amongst Chelsea fans. It was his last minute goal to give his side a chance of winning on penalties. Drogba placed the ball on the spot and took three steps back. He waited for the referee to blow his whistle. Neuer was bouncing around on his line trying to make himself as big as he could. The Chelsea striker ran up to the ball and hit it towards the bottom left corner. The German goalkeeper had guessed wrong, diving the wrong the way, and Drogba, Lampard, et al knew that this time they had done it. Chelsea were champions of Europe! Some fans ran on the pitch to celebrate and were embraced by players during the greatest achievement in the club's history.

Despite John Terry's suspension UEFA allowed him to go up and lift the trophy with Frank Lampard. At last, a Chelsea team had got their hands on Europe's greatest football trophy. The Blues owner Roman Abramovich lifted the trophy and also the relief on his quest for Champions League glory that started almost ten years previous. Roberto Di Matteo was thrown in the air by his team and then the celebrations well and truly began. There was an interesting interview on foreign TV with David Luiz where the Brazilian defender almost seemed drunk.

There would be no rest for the team as they jetted back to England. They took part in an open top bus parade around the Stamford Bridge area where tens of thousands packed the streets to get a glimpse of their new heroes and the Champions League trophy. John Terry and Frank Lampard addressed the crowd and were even pelted with celery during that time. "Champions of Europe, we'll sing it again!". Oh, and also, Chelsea winning the Champions League meant that fourth placed Tottenham were pushed out of next season's competition and into the Europa League.

GAME 88
Goal line technology

Chelsea 3 Monterrey 1
13th December 2012

FIFA Club World Cup Semi-Final
International Stadium
Chelsea; Petr Cech, Branislav Ivanovic, Ashley Cole, David Luiz (Frank Lampard 63), Fernando Torres (Victor Moses 79), Juan Mata (Paulo Ferreira 74), Oscar, John Mikel Obi, Eden Hazard, Gary Cahill, Cesar Azpilicueta
Scorers; Mata, Torres, Chavez (O.G)
Manager; Rafa Benitez
Referee; Carlos Vera
Attendance; 36,648

The 2012/13 season was the largest in Chelsea history in terms of games played. A reward for winning the Champions League was UEFA Supercup match against Atletico Madrid and entry in the FIFA's World Club Cup, held in Japan. Another bonus was that the much wanted superstar Eden Hazard announced he would be signing for the champions of Europe. He was joined by Brazilian midfielder Oscar and Spanish defender Cesar Azpilicueta.

The Blues faced Monterrey from Mexico in the semi finals of the World Club Cup. Mexico had just won the 2012 Olympic football gold medal after beating Brazil in the final which included Oscar in it's starting XI. Around a thousand Chelsea fans had made the long, 6,000 mile trip from London although many local Japanese football fans were supporting Chelsea on the day.

The Blues team selection for the game saw David Luiz employed in an unfamiliar midfield role. The debate about whether he was a better defender or midfielder went on throughout the whole season. However, it was Juan Mata whose name was on the scoresheet first. His left footed shot from just inside the box gave Chelsea a 1-0 lead heading into half time.

After the break Fernando Torres made it 2-0 within a minute of the restart and an own goal by Darvin Chavez made it 3-0 two minutes later. Monterrey did manage a consolation goal when Aldo De Nigris' effort beat Petr Cech.

The result meant they would be in the World Club Cup Final against Corinthians from Brazil. Unfortunately, Jose Paolo Guerrero's header was the only goal of the game. Gary Cahill was sent off in the final minute to dampen the mood amongst the Blues fans who had made the long journey. However, the game against Monterrey was the first time Chelsea had played in a game that involved goalline technology.

GAME 89
Ball boy bust up

Swansea 0 Chelsea 0
23rd January 2013

League Cup Semi-Final (2nd leg)
Liberty Stadium
Chelsea; Petr Cech, Branislav Ivanovic (David Luiz 68), Ashley Cole (Ryan Bertrand 86), Ramires, Frank Lampard, Juan Mata, Oscar (Fernando Torres 81), Eden Hazard, Gary Cahill, Cesar Azpilicueta, Demba Ba
Sent off; Hazard
Manager; Rafa Benitez
Referee; Chris J Foy
Attendance; 19,506

Eden Hazard was hot property. He was playing at Lille alongside former blue Joe Cole during the 2011/12 season. Cole had been singing the praises of the Belgian attacker and probably put in a good word about Chelsea as he joined the Blues at the end of the summer. In his first full season in the Premier League he made the PFA team of the year.

Chelsea were looking to add more silverware to their trophy cabinet and stood a good chance as they were drawn against Swansea in the League Cup semi final. In the first leg the Swans visited Stamford Bridge and shocked the Blues by winning 2-0. It was a poor performance but the scoreline was something that could have been overturned at the Liberty Stadium.

Chelsea fielded a strong starting XI against Swansea. However, during the first half the Blues were unable to break down the Swansea defence meaning they would need to score at least twice in the second half.

219

Unfortunately, there was a stalemate and the game ended 0-0 with Swansea earning a trip to Wembley in the League Cup final.

So why is this game memorable? With ten minutes left to play Chelsea were on the attack but Eden Hazard was unable to keep the ball in play. The referee signalled for a goalkick to be taken. A ballboy collected the ball and delayed giving it to Gerhard Tremmel in the Swansea goal. Hazard felt agitated by this and decided to take matters into his own hands. The Belgian went over to the ball boy, Charlie Morgan, aged 17, to get the ball off of him. The youngster fell on top of the ball and refused to give it to Hazard. The Chelsea attacker then started kicking the ball from underneath him. Once the ball was free the ballboy began to hold his ribs. The referee had no choice but to send Hazard off.

It later turned out that the ball boy had posted on social media that The king of all ball boys is back making his final appearance #needed #for #timewasting. It also became apparent that Charlie Morgan was the son of Swansea Director and hotel tycoon, Martin Morgan. Eden Hazard quickly apologised through Chelsea TV. After his three game suspension he scored in a 4-1 win against Wigan.

GAME 90
Frank Lampard gets the record

Aston Villa 1 Chelsea 2
11th May 2013

Premier League

Villa Park

Chelsea; Petr Cech, Ashley Cole, Ramires, Frank Lampard, Juan Mata, Victor Moses (David Luiz 45), Eden Hazard, Gary Cahill, John Terry (Branislav Ivanovic 75), Cesar Azpilicueta, Demba Ba (Fernando Torres 88)

Scorer; Lampard (2)

Sent off; Ramires

Booked; Ramires, Terry, Lampard

Manager; Rafa Benitez

Referee; Lee Mason

Attendance; 42,084

Frank Lampard is a legend of Chelsea Football Club. Some would argue he is the greatest player in the Blues history. In 2005 he came second in the Ballon D'or, behind Ronaldinho. In his time at the club he won three Premier League titles, four FA Cups, two League Cups, two Community Shields, the Europa League and of course the Champions League. On top of this he won individual awards such as the Player of Year award by the PFA, FWA, Chelsea (3 times), England (twice) and the UEFA Midfielder. He was one of the world's greatest ever midfielders.

During the 2012/13 season Frank Lampard was in negotiations with Chelsea about a new contract as his was expiring at the end of the season. Many Chelsea fans wanted him to remain at the club and Frank had said that he would also love to stay. He had given so much to the club and so his loyalty (and ability) surely deserved to be recognised. However, there was one record that Lampard was getting close to.

Back in 1907 George Hilsdon overtook Jimmy Windridge to become Chelsea leading goalscorer with 40 goals. It was another thirty years when George Mills topped the scoring charts before Roy Bentley outscored him by 1955, eventually scoring 150 goals. In 1966 England won the World Cup and a few months prior to this Bobby Tambling surpassed Bentley and scored a total of 202 goals. Kerry Dixon had come closest to eclipsing this amount but only managed 193 before moving to Southampton in 1992.

Chelsea played Stoke at the Britannia Stadium. The Blues won 4-0 and included a penalty from Frank Lampard to put his goal tally up to 194, into second place, one goal more than Kerry Dixon and just eight behind record goalscorer Bobby Tambling. Less than a week before, Steve Kutner, Lampard's agent, announced that Frank would not be offered a new contract by Chelsea and would leave when his contract expired that June. The race was on to get those eight goals.

After the Stoke game Super Frank managed to score goals against Arsenal, Reading, Newcastle, Wigan and Brentford. He was sitting on 199 goals and it was fitting that he scored his 200th Chelsea goal against his former club, West Ham. Their fans had always given him abuse for leaving the club in an £11m move in 2001. He didn't score again until the end of April when Juan Mata was brought down in the penalty area by Swansea's Leon Britton and Lampard converted from the spot. He was now just one goal away from equalling Bobby Tambling's goal scoring record which had stood since 1969. There were only a maximum of six games left before Lampard's contract was up.

In the Blues next fixture they faced Basel and won 3-1 but Lampard was not on the score sheet. A few days later they travelled to Old Trafford and beat Man Utd 1-0, with Juan Mata getting the only goal of the game. A midweek match against Tottenham came shortly after at Stamford Bridge and the home side managed a 2-2 draw but Frank was an unused substitute.

On the 11th of May Chelsea took a trip to Villa Park to take on Aston Villa. A crowd of just over 42,000 came to watch as Christian Benteke gave the Villans a 1-0 lead after 15 minutes. Ramires was later sent off before the break leaving his team to face the Villans with only ten men. The half time whistle blew and the Blues made a change with David Luiz coming on for Victor Moses.

Around the hour mark Christian Benteke was sent off for a foul on John Terry. Shortly after Frank Lampard received a pass from Eden Hazard and hit a fierce left foot shot from the edge of the area which flew past Brad Guzan in the Villa goal. He'd done it! Frank Lampard had equalled Chelsea's all time goal scoring record. What made this even more impressive was that Frank Lampard was a midfielder.

Things got even better for Chelsea and indeed Super Frank. With the final whistle fast approaching it was Hazard again who found Lampard just three yards out who couldn't miss. He had given the Blues all three points but just as importantly meant that Lampard had finally surpassed Bobby Tambling's record leaving him the top goalscorer in his own right. By the end of the season the club had taken a U-turn on their contract negotiations and Lampard agreed to sign a one year extension claiming it was always his dream to stay at Chelsea. He would then go on to score a total of 211 goals for the club and will remain a Chelsea legend forever.

GAME 91
Europa League glory

Chelsea 2 Benfica 1
15th May 2013

UEFA Europa League Final
Amsterdam Arena
Chelsea; Petr Cech, Branislav Ivanovic, Ashley Cole, David Luiz, Ramires, Frank Lampard, Fernando Torres, Juan Mata, Oscar, Gary Cahill, Cesar Azpilicueta
Scorers; Torres, Ivanovic
Booked; Oscar
Manager; Rafa Benitez
Referee; Bjorn Kuipers
Attendance; 53,000

The 2012/13 season started off well but results in the Champions League meant that Roberto Di Matteo's position as Chelsea manager was under threat. A 3-0 loss at Juventus in November was enough for the Blues board and they dismissed their manager who had won them the Champions League and FA Cup just six months previous. He was replaced by interim manager Rafa Benitez. This did not please the Chelsea faithful mainly due to his time spent at Liverpool during the Champions League battles. The supporters were very vocal about the choice of interim manager and often sang about it at games as well as filling Twitter feeds.

Chelsea finished third in their Champions League group meaning thet were eliminated from the competition but earned a place in the Europa League. It was a far cry from the heroics in Munich but none the less it was still European football with a chance of silverware, albeit with a sour taste in the mouth. First up was a tie against Sparta Prague where the Blues travelled to the Generali Arena. Oscar's goal gave Chelsea a 1-0 advantage heading into the second leg. At Stamford Bridge it was the visitors who took the lead in the 17th minute but a goal just before the final whistle from Eden Hazard earned them a match up against Steaua Bucharest.

Chelsea were drawn away in the first leg and were defeated 1-0 when Raul Rusescu won a penalty from Ryan Bertrand and scored from the resulting spot kick. The second leg saw Juan Mata get a goal back before Vlad Chiriches made it 2-1 on aggregate on the stroke of half time. However, it was the Blues who came out strongest with goals from John Terry and Fernando Torres giving them a 3-1 win on the night. Torres also missed a penalty in the last few minutes.

A 5-4 win on aggregate vs Rubin Kazan in the quarter finals meant they would play FC Basel in the semi final who had just beaten Tottenham in a penalty shootout in the quarter final. Chelsea went to St Jakob Park in the first game and looked to have won 1-0 until Cesar Azpilicueta conceded a penalty in the last five minutes of the game. Fabian Schar put it past Petr Cech to equalise on the night but a late goal from David Luiz gave the Blues a 2-1 advantage. In the return leg future CFC player Mohamed Salah scored just before half time. However, three second half goals from Torres, Moses and Luiz ensured a trip to the Amsterdam Arena to face Benfica in the final.

Before the game there was some strange debate about whether Chelsea fans wanted their team to win or not. Whilst the vast majority wanted to see their side win a trophy that their club had never lifted there were some that didn't want to have interim manager, Rafa Benitez, remembered in history as a cup winning manager. The Spaniard also didn't have a fully fit team for the final. Captain John Terry, who missed the Champions League final last year, sustained an ankle injury in the previous game meaning he was unavailable and Eden Hazard also pulled a hamstring. Not only that but this was the Blues 68th game of the season! Benfica had former and future Blues midfielder Nemanja Matic in their side.

The first half ended goalless. In the second half it was Chelsea striker Fernando Torres who broke the deadlock. His easy finish after going around Artur in the Benfica goal gave his side the lead after an hour. However, less than ten minutes later Azpilicueta was adjudged to have handballed in the area and referee Bjorn Kuipers from Holland pointed to the spot. Oscar Cardozo scored the resulting penalty and for a third consecutive European final it looked like Chelsea would need at least extra time to determine the outcome, especially as Frank Lampard saw his 87th minute strike hit the crossbar.

In the 90th minute Chelsea won a corner. Juan Mata went over to take it and cross the ball deep into the Benfica box and his ball was met by an unmarked Branislav Ivanovic who headed back across the goal and into the back of the net. His goal sent his fans into a frenzy as they had surely won another European trophy. Shortly after the referee blew his whistle and Rafa Benitez's men had won the Europa League trophy. Just like Munich, John Terry and Frank Lampard lifted the trophy together.

The win meant that Chelsea became the first ever club to win the European Cup and Europa League in consecutive seasons. The Blues also joined Juventus, Bayern Munich and Ajax in being the only clubs to have won the four main European trophies; Champions League, Europa League, Cup Winners Cup and the Super Cup.

GAME 92
Number one is Petr Cech

Hull City 0 Chelsea 2
11th January 2014

Premier League
KC Stadium
Chelsea; Petr Cech, Ashley Cole, David Luiz, Ramires (Michael Essien 90), Fernando Torres, Oscar (John Mikel Obi 79), Eden Hazard, Willian (Andre Schurrle 88), Gary Cahill, John Terry, Cesar Azpilicueta
Scorers; Hazard, Torres
Booked; Cahill
Manager; Jose Mourinho
Referee; Mark Clattenburg
Attendance; 24,924

Petr Cech was one of the best goalkeepers in the history of the Premier League. His headgear, heroics in Munich and ability meant he is arguably Chelsea's greatest ever goalkeeper. There are some older fans who will say that accolade should go to 'The Cat' Peter Bonetti.

Cech had signed for the Blues from Rennes in 2004 for £7m. Manager Claudio Ranieri wanted him to be an understudy for Carlo Cudicini who had recently been named the Chelsea Player of the Year and won ITV's Goalkeeper of the Year award. Cech did not join the club until July 2004 and by that time Ranieri had been relieved of his duties. It was up to new manager Jose Mourinho whether to stick with Cudicini or make the 22 year old his first choice keeper.

On the first day of the 2004/05 season Mourinho put his faith in Cech, giving him his debut in a 1-0 win over Man Utd. In his first eight games he only conceded once, a first minute goal from James Beattie for Southampton, although the striker did also score an own goal in the same game as Chelsea won 2-1. Cech only conceded thirteen league goals all season in 36 games.

By 2008 Petr Cech had established himself as one of the best goalkeepers in the world. On the 1st of November Chelsea welcomed Sunderland to Stamford Bridge. The Blues trashed the visitors 5-0 which included a hattrick from Nicolas Anelka. The result meant that Big Pete became only the second goalkeeper to keep 100 clean sheets for the club. The only other person to do this was Bonetti who set the record of 208 clean sheets against Wolves in 1978.

Fast forward five years to the beginning of the 2013/14 season and Petr Cech was still Chelsea's first choice. Thibaut Courtois signed for the Blues in 2011 but was loaned out to Atletico Madrid for three years. At the end of August Jose Mourinho, back in charge of Chelsea for a second time, took his side to Old Trafford. The score ended 0-0 giving Cech his 200th clean sheet. He was only eight behind goalkeeping legend Peter Bonetti who managed to keep 208 clean sheets in 729 games. By comparison, Cech had kept 200 clean sheets in just 435 matches.

Chelsea travelled to Hull City for a Premier League clash in 2014. The Blues had beaten the Tigers 2-0 on the opening day of the season with goals from Oscar and Frank Lampard. This time it was the same scoreline but with different goalscorers. Eden Hazard gave his side the lead with a shot from the edge of the box. With just a few minutes left to play Fernando Torres met a ball from Willian and netted from 12 yards out. The win briefly put Chelsea back at the top of the table but it was the clean sheet that gained the most attention. The shut out from Petr Cech meant that he had overtaken Bonetti's clean sheet record by keeping his 209th in a Blues shirt.

By the end of his Chelsea career Petr Cech had kept 227 clean sheets, won the Champions League, Europa League, Premier League (4), FA Cup (4),

League Cup (3), Community Shield (2), Premier League Golden Glove (3), Czech Footballer of the Year (8), the Chelsea Player of the Year and many other awards.

GAME 93
Triumph over Tottenham

Chelsea 2 Tottenham 0
1st March 2015

League Cup Final
Wembley
Chelsea; Petr Cech, Branislav Ivanovic, Cesc Fabregas (Oscar 88), Kurt Zouma, Ramires, Eden Hazard, Diego Costa (Didier Drogba 90), Willian (Juan Cuadrado 76), Gary Cahill, John Terry, Cesar Azpilicueta
Scorers; Terry, Costa
Booked; Willian, Cahill, Cuadrado
Manager; Jose Mourinho
Referee; Anthony Taylor
Attendance; 89,294

In 1967 Chelsea made the FA Cup final for the second time in their history. Their opponents were North London rivals Tottenham. A crowd of 100,000 people packed Wembley Stadium. It was dubbed the 'Cockney Cup Final' as it was the first to feature two London teams. Ron Harris captained the Blues to become the youngest ever captain in an FA Cup final. Bobby Tambling scored for Chelsea but his header was only a consolation goal as Spurs had already scored twice and so Tommy Docherty's men were still looking to win an FA Cup.

In 2008 there was a League Cup final between Chelsea and Tottenham at the new Wembley. The Blues were riding a wave of trophy laden success and were favourites to win the cup especially as they beat Arsenal in the previous final and Man Utd in the FA Cup final. As always, Didier Drogba scored his obligatory cup final goal in the first half direct from a freekick. However, his goal was cancelled out when Wayne Bridge conceded a penalty that was converted by Dimitar Berbatov. The game went into extra time and Jonathan Woodgate headed home from a freekick to give Spurs the trophy.

In 2014/15 Chelsea had reached the League Cup final again after beating Liverpool in the semi final when Branislav Ivanovic headed home Willian's freekick in extra time. Tottenham had beaten Sheffield United, who were playing in Engalnd's third tier, to set up the third cup final between The Blues and Spurs.

Nemanja Matic was suspended for the final after receiving a red card for pushing over Burnley's Ashley Barnes in the previous match. Fellow midfielder John Mikel Obi was also unavailable due to a knee injury. This left Chelsea short in the centre of the pitch. In the end Jose Mourinho made a surprise decision to play central defender Kurt Zouma in the middle of midfield.

The referee Anthony Taylor blew his whistle to start the game. Tottenham came close to opening the scoring when Christian Eriksen hit the crossbar from a freekick. But at the end of the first half Chelsea won their own freekick. Willian's ball was played down by Zouma and the Blues captain John Terry was on hand to hit a shot past Hugo Lloris via a deflection from Eric Dier. Ten minutes into the second half Diego Costa doubled his side's lead with a left footed shot which again was deflected into the net. The score ended 2-0 to Chelsea.

The result meant that Chelsea had earned a place in the Europa League for the following season. However, the Blues later managed to qualify for the Champions League. At the third time of asking Chelsea finally beat Tottenham in a cup final, much to the enjoyment of their fans who were truly the kings of the capital.

GAME 94
Champions again

Chelsea 1 Crystal Palace 0
3rd May 2015

Premier League
Stamford Bridge
Chelsea; Thibaut Courtois, Branislav Ivanovic, Cesc Fabregas, Eden Hazard (Filipe Luis 90), Didier Drogba, Nemanja Matic, Willian (Kurt Zouma 85), Gary Cahill, John Terry, Cesar Azpilicueta, Juan Cuadrado (John Mikel Obi 46)
Scorer; Hazard
Booked; Ivanovic, Terry
Manager; Jose Mourinho
Referee; Kevin Friend
Attendance; 41,566

Jose Mourinho had created such a buzz around Stamford Bridge when he first arrived at the club in 2004. He went on to win two Premier League titles, two League Cups, an FA Cup and a Community Shield before being sacked in 2007. The Portuguese coach then joined Inter Milan in the summer of 2008 and, just like he did with Porto in 2004, he guided his side to an unexpected Champions League victory. In 2010 he took charge of Spanish giants Real Madrid until 2013.

In June 2013 Chelsea announced that Mourinho would again be the club's manager. He began by saying he'd had two great passions in his career, Inter and Chelsea, but it was the Blues who were more important to him. Fans and pundits were giving Chelsea serious title ambitions after his re-appointment.

The 2013/14 season saw Chelsea run close to winning silverware as they reached the semi-final of the Champions League and finished four points behind champions Manchester City in the league. In February 2014 Mourinho was interviewed and said that the title race was between two horses (Arsenal and Man City) and a little horse that needs milk and needs to learn how to jump and that maybe the following year the Blues could win the race.

Chelsea started the 2014/15 season with a 3-1 win away at Burnley. Andre Schurrle scored one of the goals of the season in that game. There were debuts for Thibaut Courtois, Cesc Fabregas and Diego Costa. The win put the Blues top of the league after their first game of the season. They went on to win seven of their first eight league games. The only blip was a 1-1 draw with title rivals Man City whose goalscorer was substitute and Chelsea legend Frank Lampard who had just left the club in the summer.

Up until December Chelsea remained unbeaten in the league before Newcastle defeated Mourinho's men 2-1. They didn't lose again until Tottenham won a goal-fest on New Year's day with Spurs winning 5-3 at White Hart Lane. The Blues did get their revenge when they beat them 2-0 in the League Cup final in March.

Towards the end of the season Chelsea beat title rivals Manchester Utd 1-0 with the only goal coming from Eden Hazard. With six games left to play they found themselves ten points clear of nearest rivals and their next opponents, Arsenal. It wasn't long until Chelsea's magic number was being talked about. This was the minimum number of points they needed to win the league either by points gained or opponents dropping points. Chelsea's magic number was 9. The game at the Emirates ended 0-0 and the Blues were still ten points clear. The magic number now stood at six. The Blues headed to Leicester but found themselves 1-0 down at half time. However, a second half blitz saw the visitors win 3-1 courtesy of goals from Didier Drogba, John Terry and Ramires. The result meant that Chelsea were just three points away from guaranteeing them the league title for the first time since 2010.

Chelsea welcomed Crystal Palace to Stamford Bridge for a London derby. There was a lot of excitement and anticipation around the ground as the Blues looked to get all three points and be crowned Premier League champions for the 2014/15 season. Before the game there was a bit of drama as midfielder Ramires declared himself unavailable during the warm up and was replaced by Juan Cuadrado in the starting line-up.

Eden Hazard had been named as the PFA Player of the Year and it was the Belgian who was at the centre of the result. Just before half time the Chelsea attacker headed into the Crystal Palace penalty area and felt some slight contact from James McArthur and went down theatrically. Referee Kevin Friend pointed to the spot and it was Hazard who stepped up to take it. All the Chelsea fans were on their feet just willing him to score. Unfortunately, they were disappointed when Hazard had his penalty saved by Julian Speroni in the Palace goal. The fans quickly turned ecstatic as it was the penalty taker who reacted first and headed home the rebound. Stamford Bridge went wild!

Chelsea won the game 1-0 and earned all three points. This meant that Jose Mourinho's men were officially crowned league champions with three games left to play. In the next game Liverpool came to Stamford Bridge and gave them a guard of honour. This accompanied a 'blue carpet' and flames bursting as the players came out to a huge reception. Chelsea started the season in first place and remained there all season.

GAME 95
John Terry wins 1,000 points

Man Utd 0 Chelsea 0
28th December 2015

Premier League

Old Trafford

Chelsea; Thibaut Courtois, Branislav Ivanovic, Kurt Zouma, Oscar (Ruben Loftus-Cheek 90), Eden Hazard, John Mikel Obi, Pedro, Nemanja Matic, Willian (Ramires 70), John Terry, Cesar Azpilicueta

Booked; Mikel, Hazard

Manager; Guus Hiddink

Referee; Martin Atkinson

Attendance; 75,275

Up until 1981 teams were only awarded two points for a win. From the 1981/82 season the Football League decided to increase this to three points. The first time Chelsea won the maximum three points was on the opening day of the season in a Division Two match at Stamford Bridge against Bolton. Colin Lee and Micky Droy scored the only goals of the game in a 2-0 win for the home side.

Ron Harris played a club record of 795 games for Chelsea and was nicknamed 'Chopper' due to his no-nonsense style of defending. He was widely recognised as one of the game's toughest ever players. Harris had come through the Chelsea youth ranks and eventually named club captain. He amassed a total of 705 points in 655 league games. In 1998 another youth product made his Blues debut. His name was John Terry and from his early performances showed he was a physical defender, similar in style to Harris. Also, like Chopper, Terry went on to be named the club captain. Not only this but he became captain for the England national side from 2006 to

2012 until the FA stripped him of the armband.

John Terry made his league debut on Boxing Day 1998 in a match against Southampton at The Dell. He came on as a substitute for Gus Poyet with the score already 2-0 in his side's favour. He earned his first three points as a Chelsea player and had to wait until the final game of the season before making another league appearance. This time he replaced Michael Duberry as Chelsea beat Derby 2-1.

Terry's first start in a Premier League game came in January 2000 before a loan spell at Nottingham Forest. By 2002 he had earned 101 points in 55 games. Two years later his points tally stood at 200 after 102 games. That quickly rose to 500 points in March 2008. Only five other players had gained more points in a Chelsea shirt. At the age of 27 John Terry was showing no signs of slowing down.

In December 2010 Chelsea drew 1-1 with Everton at Stamford Bridge. The point took JT up to 700 in his Chelsea career. The first game of 2011 saw the Blues take on Aston Villa in a six-goal thriller. The game looked as if Villa would earn all three points until Didier Drogba made it 2-2 with five minutes left to play. In the 89th minute it was Terry who looked to have given his side the win until Ciaran Clark equalised at the death. The point meant that Terry had equalled the club's points record.

Over the coming years John Terry was getting older but had never been a player that had relied on speed. He had kept himself in good health and was still competing at the top level. On the 28th of December 2015 the Blues visited Old Trafford for a match against Man Utd. Although the game ended 0-0 it did mean that John Terry had become the only player in CFC history to amass 1,000 points as a Chelsea player. By the time he ended his career at Stamford Bridge he had won 1,040 points in total, over 100 points more than his nearest rival, Frank Lampard.

GAME 96
Hazard halts Tottenham's title attempt

Chelsea 2 Tottenham 2
2nd May 2016

Premier League
Stamford Bridge
Chelsea; Asmir Begovic, Branislav Ivanovic, Cesc Fabregas, John Mikel Obi, Pedro (Eden Hazard 45), Diego Costa, Nemanja Matic (Oscar 78), Willian, Gary Cahill, John Terry, Cesar Azpilicueta
Scorers; Cahill, Hazard
Booked; Willian, Mikel
Manager; Guus Hiddink
Referee; Mark Clattenburg
Attendance; 41,545

Ask Chelsea fans which game they look out for first when the fixture list for the new season comes out and many will say Tottenham. There has always been a rivalry between the two London sides going back to their first encounter back in 1909 with the Blues winning 2-1 courtesy of goals from Jimmy Windridge and James Bradshaw.

Over the years many players have represented both clubs including Jimmy Greaves, Terry Venables, Jason Cundy, Graham Roberts, Micky Hazard, Gustavo Poyet, Gordon Durie, William Gallas and Glenn Hoddle. The latter had also managed both sides in his career.

In the 2014/15 season Chelsea were crowned champions but after a terrible following campaign the Blues were hovering around mid-table. Tottenham were on a winning run and were part of a two horse race to win the Premier League. On the 2nd of May 2016 Spurs came to Stamford Bridge to try to

CHELSEA: 100 MEMORABLE MATCHES

keep up with surprise league leaders, Leicester City. In the previous 154 meetings between the two London rivals it was Chelsea who had the better record, although Spurs had done better in cup finals. Despite their mid-table position the Blues had not lost to Tottenham at Stamford Bridge since 1990, a run lasting 28 games!

The match gained lots of media attention as Spurs needed to win all three points in order to stay in the title race. A draw or loss would ensure Leicester, managed by former Chelsea boss Claudio Ranieri, would be Premier League champions. TV cameras were set up in order to show Leicester fans reactions throughout the game.

It didn't look like Chelsea would do Leicester any favours as Tottenham struck first after 35 minutes through Harry Kane. To make things worse Son Heung-Min made it 2-0 just before half time and it seemed as though they had finally beaten the Stamford Bridge hoo doo. At half time manager Guus Hiddink decided to bring on Eden Hazard for Pedro. The Belgian had only made one league appearance in almost two months.

Just before the hour mark the Blues won a corner at the Shed End. The ball found Gary Cahill and he hit a left footed shot past Hugo Lloris in the Spurs goal. Now there was some hope for Hiddink's men to continue their unbeaten streak against their opponents. However, as time ticked on Spurs refused to be broken down. They did however have a bit of a meltdown in terms of discipline and nine of their players received a yellow card by the end of the match.

With less than ten minutes to go Eden Hazard received the ball in his own half. He decided to take on a couple of Spurs players before passing it to Diego Costa. The Spanish striker managed to out-muscle a Tottenham defender before laying the ball into the path of Hazard. Without hesitation the Belgian struck a first time shot from the edge of the box which curled into the top corner and sent football fans around the world into a frenzy.

Not only was it a spectacular goal, it kept the Blues unbeaten record in tact. Also, TV showed videos of Leicester fans watching the game and they were overcome with joy and excitement as the 2-2 draw meant they were crowned champions.

Eden Hazard was Chelsea's hero the previous season and in 2015/16 he became hero again when his goal officially ended Tottenham's chances of winning the league. Despite it being a two-horse race, Spurs actually finished third as Arsenal pipped them to the runners-up spot. It was a game filled with drama and emotion but it was relief that was the greatest feeling that Chelsea fans experienced as Tottenham would have to wait even longer to win their first league title since 1961.

GAME 97
The untouchables

Chelsea 4 Man Utd 0
23rd October 2016

Premier League
Stamford Bridge
Chelsea; Thibaut Courtois, Marcos Alonso, N'Golo Kante, Eden Hazard (Willian 78), Pedro (Nathaniel Chalobah 71), Victor Moses, Diego Costa (Michy Batshuayi 78), Nemanja Matic, Gary Cahill, Cesar Azpilicueta, David Luiz
Scorers; Pedro, Cahill, Hazard, Kante
Booked; Pedro, Luiz, Alonso
Manager; Antonio Conte
Referee; Martin Atkinson
Attendance; 41,424

In May 2015 Chelsea had just won the Premier League under Jose Mourinho's leadership. By Christmas the Blues and the Portuguese manager had parted company by mutual consent. The Jose the Chelsea fans had seen in recent years was not the same one they fell in love with ten years before. He had begun to split opinions among fans, with some saying he'd lost it and some demanding respect for the man that gave them so many trophies and great memories during his tenure.

At the end of the 2015/16 season Chelsea finished tenth in the league, a huge drop from being champions just twelve months before. Jose Mourinho then signed a three year contract with Manchester United and his new team, alongside Man City's new manager Pep Guardiola, were made joint favourites to win the league in 2017. Jose's start at United included winning the Community Shield against Leicester.

In October 2016 Chelsea welcomed Man Utd to Stamford Bridge. Jose Mourinho returned with his backroom team which included so many former Blues coaching staff. Before the game Chelsea were sitting in fifth whilst Man Utd were in 7th. The question was what type of performance would the visitors put in? Would they go all out attack or would they park the bus, a defensive strategy synonymous with Mourinho even from his Chelsea days.

Referee Martin Atkinson blew his whistle to signal the start of the game as Chelsea kicked off. Diego Costa stood in the centre circle and passed it back into midfield. The ball was then played around the Chelsea defence before Marcos Alonso hit the ball forward towards the Man Utd penalty box. Two reds defenders were not concentrating but Pedro was for the Blues. He took one touch round David De Gea on the edge of the box and a second touch to slot the ball into an open net. Chelsea had started off by scoring after just 30 seconds. This was not the club's fastest ever goal, not even their quickest in the Premier League, but what did make this goal different was that the Blues were 1-0 up without the opposition even touching the ball!

Later in the game there were goals from Gary Cahill, Eden Hazard and N'Golo Kante with the home side running out 4-0 winners against Jose Mourinho's side. Instead of the fans chanting Mourinho's name, there was a new guy in town. Antonio Conte was now the Blues boss after leaving the Italian national side in the summer. The other name being chanted was that of former board member, Matthew Harding. It was the 20th anniversary since his death and all the usual banners around the ground were removed, leaving just those referring to Harding visible. He would have been proud of his team and their performance.

GAME 98
Conte's men crowned champions

West Brom 0 Chelsea 1
12th May 2017

Premier League

The Hawthorns

Chelsea; Thibaut Courtois, Marcos Alonso, Cesc Fabregas, Eden Hazard (Willian 75), Pedro (Michy Batshuayi 75), Victor Moses (Kurt Zouma 86), Diego Costa, Nemanja Matic, Gary Cahill, Cesar Azpilicueta, David Luiz

Scorer; Batshuayi

Manager; Antonio Conte

Referee; Michael Oliver

Attendance; 25,367

Antonio Conte was the Italian national team manager heading into the 2016 European Championships but had already decided to leave this post at the end of the competition to become Chelsea's new boss. He had previously been in charge of Juventus and competed against the Blues in the 2012/13 Champions League group stage. The game at Stamford Bridge ended 2-2 but the game in Turin ended 3-0 to the Old Lady. This turned out to be Roberto Di Matteo's last game as Chelsea boss.

The summer of 2016 was a merry-go-round for managerial changes. Southampton, Everton, Watford, Hull and Chelsea made pre-season appointments. However, these were less profile than the changes in Manchester. Louis van Gaal was sacked as Man Utd's boss and replaced by Jose Mourinho. The blue side of Manchester had appointed Pep Guardiola, the man behind Barcelona and Bayern Munich's recent success. There was a media frenzy around the couple and many believed the Premier League champions would come from one of these two clubs.

Antonio Conte began his tenure as the Blues boss with a 2-1 win vs West Ham. Eden Hazard had given Chelsea the lead from the penalty spot but James Collins equalised with a header. However, Diego Costa scored from the edge of the box at the end of the game to seal all three points. The Chelsea fans reaction was only bettered by their new manager's. He turned to the crowd, showed his passion and jumped in with them. After just one game the supporters (and media) were in love with his celebrations.

As the season continued there were many other celebrations but things took a turn for the worse by the end of September as the Blues slumped to a 2-1 defeat against Liverpool and a humiliating 3-0 loss at Arsenal. The Italian manager decided that it was time for a change. Instead of employing the usual 4-2-3-1 formation the team had been used to playing, he switched to three at the back. The impact was almost unbelievable as they went on a run of six consecutive league wins without conceding a single goal. In fact, they only let in two goals until after Boxing Day. At this point his team were top of the table, seven points clear of nearest rivals Man City. Jose Mourinho's side were 13 points behind.

In April 2017 Chelsea had to play both Man City and Man Utd. First they welcomed Pep Guardiola to Stamford Bridge and ran out 2-1 winners courtesy of an Eden Hazard brace either side of Sergio Aguero's strike. However, it wasn't as pleasing at Old Trafford as Marcus Rashford and Ander Herrera scored the only goals of the game in a 2-0 defeat. With six games left it was Chelsea leading the pack with Tottenham their closest rivals. The Blues magic number was 15. By the end of April it was down to nine points.

Chelsea were ready to face West Brom at The Hawthorns. This had become a bit of a bogey ground in recent seasons but due to Spurs' loss at West Ham it meant that a win for the Blues would guarantee them the Premier League crown. Fans anticipated that this would be the night where their team would be champions again, especially as they had scored 14 goals in the last four games.

Chelsea were almost awarded a penalty in the first half when the ball appeared to have hit Chris Brunt on the arm but the lack of chances were frustrating and the half ended 0-0. With only fifteen minutes to go it was still goalless and Antonio Conte decided to make a double change. Off came Pedro and Hazard to be replaced by Willian and Michy Batshuayi. This was a more attacking change although somewhat strange to bring off Hazard and bring on his Belgian team mate. Batshuayi had signed in the summer for £33m from Marseille but had struggled to make any impact in the league. His last goal came from the penalty spot in January against Brentford in the FA Cup. Michy's only goal in the Premier League came in August during the second game of the season.

In the 82nd minute Chelsea were on the attack. Cesar Azpilicueta had pushed forward and chased the ball to stop it from going out. His cross from near the touchline found Michy Batshuayi unmarked in the six yard box and the striker easily slotted in past Ben Foster. A knee slide celebration followed before the Chelsea players jumped on top of him. It was the goal that sealed the trophy for Antonio Conte's men and Chelsea were Premier League champions with two games to spare. The final couple of matches saw the Blues win 4-3 against Watford and 5-1 vs Sunderland with Michy scoring twice in each game.

Man City ended the season in third place, fifteen points behind whilst Jose Mourinho could only manage to finish 6th, a massive 24 points away from his former club. It was Antonio Conte who had earned all the plaudits by winning Manager of the Month on three consecutive months and the manager of the season award. N'Golo Kante, Chelsea's summer signing, won the Player of the Year trophy. He joined Eden Hazard, David Luiz and Gary Cahill in the PFA team of the year.

GAME 99
First winners at Wembley

Tottenham 1 Chelsea 2
20th August 2017

Premier League
Wembley
Chelsea; Thibaut Courtois, Antonio Rudiger, Marcos Alonso, N'Golo Kante, Alvaro Morata (Michy Batshuayi 79), Tiemoue Bakayoko, Victor Moses, Willian (Pedro 78), Andreas Christensen, Cesar Azpilicueta, David Luiz
Scorer; Alonso (2)
Booked; Rudiger, Luiz, Alonso
Manager; Antonio Conte
Referee; Anthony Taylor
Attendance; 73,587

Wembley is arguably the most famous and iconic football stadium in the world. It first opened to the public in 1923 but was known as the British Empire Exhibition Satdium. It was built by Sir Robert McAlpine and was made for the exhibition of 1924. The cost of the stadium was £750,000 and was originally meant to be demolished when the exhibition finished. However, the stadium was saved and used as the new home for the FA Cup final.

The FA Cup final was held in different stadiums in its time and prior to Wembley the last three finals were played at Stamford Bridge. The winners in that time were Aston Villa, Huddersfield Town and Tottenham. Up until the year 2000 every FA Cup had been won at Wembley with the exception of one, when Chelsea beat Leeds Utd in 1970 at Old Trafford.

It wasn't just the FA Cup final that was synonymous with Wembley as

England won the 1966 World Cup at the same ground. This was in addition to European Cup finals and the Olympics. Football legend, Pele, once described Wembley as the cathedral of football. It was every player's dream to play at the stadium and for every fan to watch their team there. There was no bigger event than playing at Wembley.

Despite all the big games Wembley had never been used for a Premier League fixture. That was until Tottenham decided to rebuild White Hart Lane and needed a temporary ground. The FA agreed that Spurs could use it during the building works and had already played some Champions League games at the stadium.

In the 2017-18 season Tottenham started their league campaign away to Newcastle and won 2-0. Their next game was the much anticipated match-up against Chelsea for the first ever Premier League game played at Wembley. A crowd of over 73,000 came to watch the spectacle. Chelsea had made a few signings in the summer including Antonio Rudiger, Tiemoue Bakayoko and record transfer Alvaro Morata.

The game started off well for Chelsea when David Luiz was fouled by Dele Alli 25 yards out. Marcos Alonso stood over the ball and bent it superbly into the net past Hugo Lloris to put the Blues 1-0 up. The score remained the same by half time. With around ten minutes to go Antonio Conte made a change with Michy Batshuayi replacing Morata up front. It only took a few minutes for the Belgian striker to make an impact. Sadly for Chelsea it just happened to be a header into his own net and Tottenham were level.

The game appeared to be heading for a draw until the 88th minute when Pedro dribbled with the ball and passed it to Alonso who was making a forward run into the box. His first time shot went underneath the Spurs keeper to send the travelling fans into celebration. There has always been something so satisfying in seeing Chelsea beat Tottenham and this was no different. The Blues ran out 2-1 winners and made history by being the first ever team to win a Premier League game at Wembley.

GAME 100
A trophy to end the season

Chelsea 1 Man Utd 0
19th May 2018

FA Cup Final
Wembley
Chelsea; Thibaut Courtois, Antonio Rudiger, Marcos Alonso, Cesc Fabregas, N'Golo Kante, Eden Hazard (Willian 90), Tiemoue Bakayoko, Victor Moses, Olivier Giroud (Alvaro Morata 89), Gary Cahill, Cesar Azpilicueta
Scorer; Hazard
Booked; Courtois
Manager; Antonio Conte
Referee; Michael Oliver
Attendance; 87,647

The FA Cup has created so many great memories for Chelsea fans, players and managers alike. It's not just been winning the cup that has been memorable but also the journey they took to try and reach the final. Some of the memories will be remembered forever although others will want to be forgotten. The 2017/18 season had both of these elements.

Chelsea had won the Premier League in the previous season breaking all kinds of records along the way but were unable to win the double as they lost to Arsenal in the FA Cup final. The next season was going well at first and the club were sitting in second place towards the end of the year. However, some inconsistent performances and results saw the Blues slip down the table. It also seemed like Antonio Conte was starting to lose his warmth, passion and interest in the job.

As the season continued, or some would say dragged on, tensions were being felt amongst supporters, players and the media with Conte at the heart of it all. Despite that, Chelsea did manage to reach the FA Cup semi-final against Southampton. The winner would play either Tottenham or Man Utd in the final.

A week before the semi-final the Blues took on Southampton at St Mary's Stadium. It was the home side who took the lead in the first half and doubled their lead on the hour mark. At this point Chelsea made a double substitution with Davide Zappacosta and Alvaro Morata being replaced by Pedro and Olivier Giroud. Ten minutes later Giroud gave his side hope by getting a goal back. Within the next eight minutes goals from Eden Hazard and Giroud put the Blues ahead and won 3-2. It was a comeback that was not on the cards.

In the semi-final Giroud had earned a place in the starting line-up at the expense of Morata. The Frenchman justified his place by scoring early in the second half. He was later swapped with Morata and this time it was the Spanish striker who scored after coming off the bench. The 2-0 scoreline didn't change and Antonio Conte's men were in the final against Man Utd.

In previous FA Cup finals between Chelsea and Man Utd both had tasted victory. In 1994 it was the reds who won the cup in a 4-0 win in which some controversial refereeing lead to Eric Cantona scoring two penalties. In 2007 it was the Blues who won courtesy of a Didier Drogba goal in extra time to win the first FA Cup final at the new Wembley.

The FA Cup final took place on the 19th May 2018, exactly six years after Chelsea won the Champions League. The European win seemed like only yesterday to many fans but the reality of winning it again was a lot further away especially as they had failed to qualify for next season's competition.

The game was cagey and both sides were out not to lose. Jose Mourinho was famous for parking the bus in big games and Conte's men were coming off of not qualifying for Europe's biggest prize. Whereas in previous years the FA Cup final was a game of anticipation and excitement, this one seemed like just another game. The quality of the game was put into question after the match. It was in fact Chelsea who won the cup after Eden Hazard scored a first half penalty. The Belgian won the spot kick when he was fouled by Phil Jones, who was lucky to escape a red card.

The win meant that the Blues had won the FA Cup for an eighth time. Only Man Utd and Arsenal had won the FA Cup more than this. There was much speculation that this was Antonio Conte's last game in charge of Chelsea and would be sacked the following day. However, that day did not come until part way through pre-season where he was replaced by a fellow Italian, Maurizio Sarri.

Your memorable match

Use this part of the book to write about one of your memorable matches. Maybe it was the first game you went to, the first time you took one of your children, a match of great importance, excitement or even disappointment. This is a chance to pass on your own memorable match for the next generation of Chelsea fans.

Score;

....

Date;

....

Competition;

....

Venue;

....

Chelsea line-up;

....

....

....

....

Scorer(s);

....

Booking(s);

....

Manager;

....

Referee;

....

Attendance;

....

GATE 17
THE COMPLETE COLLECTION
(NOVEMBER 2018)

FOOTBALL
Over Land and Sea - Mark Worrall
Chelsea here, Chelsea There - Kelvin Barker, David Johnstone, Mark Worrall
Chelsea Football Fanzine - the best of cfcuk
One Man Went to Mow - Mark Worrall
Chelsea Chronicles (Five Volume Series) - Mark Worrall
Making History Not Reliving It - Kelvin Barker, David Johnstone, Mark Worrall
Celery! Representing Chelsea in the 1980s - Kelvin Barker
Stuck On You: a year in the life of a Chelsea supporter - Walter Otton
Palpable Discord: a year of drama and dissent at Chelsea - Clayton Beerman
Rhyme and Treason - Carol Ann Wood
Eddie Mac Eddie Mac - Eddie McCreadie's Blue & White Army
The Italian Job: A Chelsea thriller starring Antonio Conte - Mark Worrall
Carefree! Chelsea Chants & Terrace Culture - Mark Worrall, Walter Otton
Diamonds, Dynamos and Devils - Tim Rolls
Arrivederci Antonio: The Italian Job (part two) - Mark Worrall
Where Were You When We Were Shocking? - Neil L. Smith
Chelsea: 100 Memorable Games – Chelsea Chadder

FICTION
Blue Murder: Chelsea till I die - Mark Worrall
The Wrong Outfit - Al Gregg
The Red Hand Gang - Walter Otton
Coming Clean - Christopher Morgan
This Damnation - Mark Worrall
Poppy - Walter Otton

NON FICTION
Roe2Ro - Walter Otton
Shorts - Walter Otton

www.gate17.co.uk

Printed in Great Britain
by Amazon

36283325R00158